ROGER DUVAL

Retirement Base Camp: Mapping out the RIGHT Financial Future
Copyright © 2018 Roger Duval

BMD Publishing
All Rights Reserved

ISBN # 978-1724662781

BMD Publishing CEO: Seth Greene
Editorial Management: Bruce Corris
Cover Art & Layout: Kristin Watt

BMDPublishing@MarketDominationLLC.com
MarketDominationLLC.com

Sale of this book without a front cover may be unauthorized. If this book is coverless, it may have been reported to the publisher as "unsold or destroyed" and neither the author nor the publisher has received payment for it.

No part of this publication may be reproduced, stored in a retrieval system, or transmitted in any form or by any means, electronic, mechanical, photocopying, recording, or otherwise, without the prior written permission of the Publisher. Requests to the Publisher for permission should be sent to BMD Publishing, 5888 Main Street, Suite 100, Williamsville, NY 14221.

Printed in the United States of America

DEDICATION

To Joe Jordan:

Because I was in an audience when you were laying bare your heart…and I decided to become an advocate for families and live a life of significance.

******

To my wife, Karen:

On the road trip from Seattle to Spokane, you listened to me and came up with the title for this book. Us forever!

INTRODUCTION

Retirement can be scary. It's all too easy to imagine yourself lost in the wilderness, struggling to find your way to the lifestyle you want.

That is, unless you have a guide.

Which is how I think of myself. Not just a financial advisor, more of a financial educator, guiding my clients on the path to security and peace of mind.

So I'll be your guide, or "Sherpa" if you will, throughout this book. I brought together this team of Spokane-area experts and professionals, because planning for retirement is so much more than making sure you have the money. It's about redefining yourself and living the lifestyle you want. There are many facets to retirement planning that most people don't think about, or don't seek help with. In a world of do-it-yourselfers, this is an area that is best approached with solid advice from experts who have seen all the "what-ifs" in life. Think about it. You wouldn't plan an expedition up Mt. Everest with just a bank account and some personal research, would you?

I put together this team of financial, legal, fitness and lifestyle experts to answer your questions, even the ones you haven't thought to ask. So no matter what life throws your way, you'll be prepared, and able to take charge of your life and health now, so you can live the life you want down the road.

This is why I am so passionate about what I do. I believe the "what-ifs" in life can be navigated with ease, with the right planning. After all, where would Everest climbers be without the aid of their Sherpas?

The people I interviewed share their knowledge, experience, and valuable insights. I hope you get as much out of reading these interviews as I did conducting them.

> *"Do not let your fire go out, spark by irreplaceable spark in the hopeless swamps of the not-quite, the not-yet, and the not-at-all. Do not let the hero in your soul perish in lonely frustration for the life you deserved and have never been able to reach. The world you desire can be won. It exists…it is real…it is possible…it is yours."*
>
> Ayn Rand, Atlas Shrugged.

Roger Duval
September 2018

CASE STUDY

17,590 feet above Katmandu, Nepal, sits the famous Base Camp where climbers get acclimated to thinning air as they make their final preparations for the ascension to the summit of Mt. Everest. These climbers have planned for this trek over a span of many years. They are in peak physical condition and have all the best equipment. They are ready for the climb, yet they still don't go it alone. They've hired professional guides, called Sherpas, who live in the high altitudes of Nepal and who possess invaluable experience when it comes to safely getting their clients to a successful summit—29,028 feet, or roughly the altitude of a commercial airline flight—and back down.

Around the age of 50, many people begin to look seriously at the daunting mountain of retirement that is approaching and they start to ask questions. Will I have enough money? How will I generate enough income to accommodate my desired lifestyle? What happens if my investments lose value at the wrong time? What happens to my family if my health takes a downturn and I need specialized care? What kind of legacy do I want to leave?

Welcome to your very own Base Camp; Retirement Base Camp. This book is packed with advice. In addition to the financial advice I will share, I've also interviewed many other professionals who will share their guidance on various topics that are important for a successful journey through retirement.

You've done some good work to get to where you are today. The real mountain, though, is now ahead of you. It's time to take inventory and check your equipment, hire your guides, and enjoy what you've worked so hard for over so many years. My chosen analogy is mountain climbing, but, in reality, your actual retirement can consist of any combination of activities. I suspect we have far more sunshine seekers than actual ice climbing mountaineers. The tools you need to succeed in retirement are the same regardless of your lifestyle. And those tools are analogous to mountain climbing. You need ascension gear, daily provisions, downside safety, and protections against the unforeseen "what ifs" that can interrupt your best laid plans.

Ascension Gear

One of my favorite investment terms is *Mountain Chart*. A mountain chart shows the historical record of an investment—such as a mutual fund—ascending from a humble beginning on the left side of a page to a much larger present-day value on the right. Let us begin our base camp lessons and retirement preparations with a discussion of stocks—essential for ascension.

Founded in 1934, the American Funds are one of the oldest and most respected families of mutual funds in the world. The Investment Company of America (ICA) is their oldest mutual fund. The ICA sales brochure has a four-page foldout illustrating my favorite mountain chart. The left corner begins with a $10,000 investment made in 1934. Following the ever-increasing mountain to the right, with no money added or withdrawn, over that 84-year timespan, the original investment would be worth over $125 million now.

https://www.americanfunds.com/advisor/pdf/broker/mfgebrx-004_icag.pdf

Of course, people don't invest that way. People invest for shorter periods of time and they eventually plan to take withdrawals and spend money…but I start with the mental picture of this mountain chart because I want you to think about all the bad stuff that has happened in the world since 1934. Wars, recessions, inflation spikes, assassinations… Practically every year there would have been some crisis, some reason for the talking heads on television to make you afraid of the big bad scary stock market. Stocks are not your enemies. One important truth I want you to know is stocks can be your friends and they are a very important part of most successful retirement plans.

What are stocks? Imagine you are holding a checkbook with an unlimited balance. Your job is to shop for a single company to buy. Once you buy that company, all of your future income and wealth will come from the goods and services provided by that company. How diligent would you be while shopping for that most excellent company?

Would you look at Boeing, a company that manufactures airplanes and participates in lucrative defense contracts? Perhaps you see all your friends, morning after morning, buying their expensive coffee concoctions so owning Starbucks would be attractive to you. Maybe you've never gotten out of Costco for under $200 and you think those cash registers should belong to you. Texting, phone calls, all the worlds knowledge in a rectangle that fits in your pocket... Apple perhaps?

That unlimited checkbook balance does not exist, but you CAN own part of these, and other publicly traded companies. You can own them through buying their stocks.

How do you make money by owning stocks? There are two main ways investors can make money through stock ownership. The first way to make money is to own stocks that are increasing their profits over time. The increased profits generally result in the price of the stock going higher.

The opposite can happen if a company has decreasing profits, or poor management. The stock price can decrease and investors can lose money.

The second way investors can earn money by owning stocks is through dividends. Dividends are generally paid quarterly and they represent a slice of the company profits. Your dividends can be reinvested in more shares or you can receive them in cash. Owning companies with long track records of increasing dividends is one of my preferred strategies for participating in the stock market.

Many investors choose to own stocks by using mutual funds or exchange traded funds (ETFs). Mutual funds are exactly what the name implies. Investors mutually fund an account that is professionally managed. Each investor owns a portion of the mutual fund. By pooling money into a mutual fund, investors can own dozens or hundreds of stocks. Spreading your money across many stocks is called diversification and mutual funds are an easy way to achieve that diversification.

ETFs are similar to mutual funds in that they offer diversification. There are some key differences between mutual funds and ETFs. ETFs are often focused on certain industries, such as health care, defense and aerospace, technology, etc. The management fees are usually quite a bit lower than mutual funds and the holdings inside the ETF are not as actively managed—frequently bought and sold—as are most mutual funds.

How you choose to own stocks (Individual companies, mutual funds, or ETFs) is not as important as the basic need *for* you to have some stock ownership in your retirement tool kit.

I can hear many of you echoing back things you've heard over the years of your life:

"Get out of stocks when you get close to retirement."

"What goes up must come down."

"October: This is one of the peculiarly dangerous months to speculate in stocks. The others are July, January, September, April, November, May, March, June, December, August and February." That one comes to us from Mark Twain.

I want you to see stocks differently. Stock ownership has played an important part in capitalism throughout history and stock ownership will play a major role in the future of capitalism. Let's look inside The Dow Jones Industrial Average (Dow) for a lesson in stock ownership and the importance of dividends.

The Dow Jones Industrial Average was first calculated and published in May of 1896. The Dow Index contained the stocks of 12 companies and the first published value was 40.94. At the writing of this book, mid 2018, the Dow represents 30 stocks and the average is quoted around 25,000. Seems like nice growth over 120 years, yes? Consider this: The Dow Jones Industrial Average does not include the historical dividend payouts of the companies inside the index. It is just a measure of price changes over time. If dividends were included in the value calculation of the Dow, instead of Dow 25,000, your nightly news program would be quoting a Dow index well north of 1 million.

Ownership creates wealth. Over time, owners of good properties, good companies and other assets become wealthier through holding those ascending assets.

Over time the costs of goods and services tend to increase. That phenomenon is referred to as inflation. Historically, stock ownership has been a pretty solid place to have your money outpace inflation. Consider the Rule of 72. An easy way to determine how many years it will take for your money to double is to divide your interest rate, or your rate of return, into 72. For example, if your bank is paying you 1% on a savings account, that money would double in 72 years. If your investment portfolio averages 10%, your money will double in 7.2 years.

Remember stories your parents would tell about how inexpensive their first house was? Or their first car? Prices of goods and services tend to increase over time. Your investments should have exposure to asset classes (stocks) that can keep pace with, or outpace, inflation. An overlooked aspect of inflation comes into play with the evolution of gadgets not yet invented. A person retiring back in 1992 probably did not include the monthly cost associated with smart phones and data plans. Why? Because those presently indispensable items did not yet exist. The technology was in its infancy, but the days of $200 per month family cell bills were not on the checklists of very many retirement plans. What things are in their infancy right now that we need to account for? One example might be self-driving cars. If self-driving cars become as ubiquitous as smart phones, those cars will add an unforeseen expense to your retirement. Always plan extra future income to pay for the unknowns.

As you go through your day, take a close look at everything you use, everything you buy, and every service you pay for. How many of those things are made available to you by companies in which you can buy stock? Your toothpaste, your clothes, the lights in your house, the car you drive, the gas in your car, the cell phone that you put away when you drive, the medicine you take, the food you eat…the list goes on. Corporations are responsible for most of the quality of life we enjoy. Corporations strive to make better products and services in a competitive effort to win our business. Yes, I know, several large "customer service" departments seem like they're on a mission to drive business away, but hopefully you get my overall point. Advances in medicine, improvements in restaurants, auto safety features, have all come about due to the profit motive of capitalism. What a great truth it is that you and I can participate in corporate profits though stock ownership.

Let me give you a very practical example of what stock ownership can do for you. How much do you pay every year to your local gas and electric company? Look up the stock of that utility company. What is the dividend payout from that stock? Next figure out how much of that stock you would have to own for that dividend to pay your utility bill. If you buy enough of that stock, your future utility bills can be paid by your local utility. Most utilities tend to be good long-term stocks to own. You could literally drive up and down your neighborhood streets passing by houses occupied by people who are paying your utility bills. They send in their monthly payments, the utility provides a service and turns a profit, some of that profit is paid out to shareholders. You, the shareholder, receive that dividend money and you use it to pay your utility bill. Thank you, neighbors. Thank you, capitalism.

There are many ways to own stocks. Some people are perfectly adept at managing their own stock portfolios. Most, though, want and need guidance. My advice to those who want help is to partner with a professional who believes in holding quality stocks for the long run. Frequent trading is usually a fool's game. Quality investments are to be held for many years. Whether you buy individual stocks, mutual funds, ETFs, or any combination of these, take some serious time at your retirement base camp to partner with a professional who has a great deal of experience and a history of successful investing.

Downside Protection and Guaranteed Provisions

The next retirement tool you should have is downside protection. While stocks do tend to go higher over long periods of time, they can also decline in value—sometimes fast and violently—and a major downturn in stocks right when you plan to retire can induce fear and cause real problems.

Traditionally, investors would use bonds to help with downside protection. There may come a day when that strategy returns to viability, but as of this writing bond yields are historically low and we are likely heading into a time when interest rates are going to head higher. When interest rates go up, bond prices go in the opposite direction; yep, down. Bonds are not ownership. Bonds represent loans made to companies and governments. In exchange for those entities using your money, they agree to pay you a coupon rate, or a yield.

When you hear talk of the United States debt, you are hearing the total of all the federal treasury bonds that are outstanding.

Those yard signs encouraging you to vote for the next school levy…When those propositions pass, bonds are issued. People with money buy the bonds, the school is built, and the bondholders receive payments while their money is being used. Property taxes incrementally go higher, and as those increasing revenues come into the school district, that money is eventually used to pay off the bonds as the bonds reach various maturity dates. This is an example of a municipal bond.

Similarly, corporate bonds are issued by companies as a way to bring in large amounts of money to fund research and development, expansions, or various other capital needs.

The yields from municipal bonds are generally tax free, while the yields from corporate bonds and treasury bonds are subject to income taxation. Bonds can be an important part of a retirement plan and the professional guide you partner with to learn about stocks can teach you about bonds as well.

Bonds tend to act differently than stocks. Bond prices can be influenced by the financial performance of the underlying issuer, but the prices of bonds tend to be most influenced by interest rates. When interest rates are at—or above—historical averages, bonds can offer some downside protection to an investment portfolio. In today's world of very low—and rising—interest rates, I prefer a different approach to downside protection.

Consider various forms of annuities when you are working with your advisor (your base camp guide) to come up with downside protection for some of your portfolio.

Let's explore some annuity strategies for downside protection. If you have a long time before retirement—10 years or more—one strategy that makes sense is to look at your investments annually and harvest some of the gains following years when your stocks have appreciated. Those harvested gains can then be used to purchase deferred income annuities.

Take our hypothetical couple, Joe and Mary. They have a $500,000 portfolio of mutual funds. The funds appreciate by 10% so now they have $550,000. If they take half of that gain and buy a deferred income annuity they will still have $525,000 and they just took an important step for future income and downside protection. Assume Joe and Mary are able to do this 6 out of 10 years with various amounts of money. For simple math, let's assume their mutual funds have averaged 8% over the 10-year period of time and they've made six different purchases into a differed income annuity totaling $150,000. After 10 years, they have a stock portfolio worth approximately $750,000. They begin taking withdrawals in retirement. They take 4% from that portfolio, or $30,000 annually. That $2,500 monthly income is not guaranteed. Historically a good mutual fund portfolio should support that rate of withdrawal. However, we all know there will come a year when their mutual fund portfolio takes a dip.

Let's give Joe and Mary 5 good years of mutual fund returns as they enter retirement. They've been taking 4% annual withdrawals and those good years have allowed them to increase their income. Their portfolio is now $850,000 and the monthly income has risen from $2,500 to $2,800. A bad year hits the stock market and their $850,000 declines to $700,000. Now, if they continue taking $2,800 per month from $700,000, they are putting extra stress on their mutual funds by withdrawing closer to 5% annually. Solution? Deploy the deferred income annuity they stashed away during the 10-year run up prior to retirement.

Joe and Mary contact their investment professional and discover that their deferred income annuity can be turned on and will provide lifetime guaranteed income of $1,000 per month.

Now, let's re-do their math. They can reduce the amount coming from their mutual funds. Set that back to 4% of the $700,000, or $2,300 per month. Add in the $1,000 protected income from the deferred income annuity and Joe and Mary get an overall <u>pay increase</u> to $3,300 per month. All this while their friends and neighbors are figuring out how to live on less money while the stock market throws one of its occasional tantrums.

An interesting feature of deferred income annuities is that the amount of guaranteed income goes up every year as you defer them. Your income goes up just because you get older and wait to turn on the income spigot. We can all do that, right?

Social Security is essentially a deferred income annuity program. You've been putting money into it over your working career and the longer you wait to begin withdrawals—up to age 70—the higher your monthly income will be for life.

In the illustration above I showed Joe and Mary buying one deferred income annuity and adding to it over time. A slightly different approach is one of my favorites. In the 10-years or so leading up to retirement, buy a separate deferred income annuity every year. During retirement, every year, for the first ten years, turn on the income from the oldest annuity. The results of this strategy are you give yourself a lifetime pay increase every single year during your initial decade in retirement.

Combine that strategy with adding a Longevity Deferred Income Annuity and you are really cooking with gas. A longevity annuity is simply a deferred income annuity that is designed to kick in at a certain age…usually 80 or older. The payouts on those annuities are very high because not every owner lives to that age. It's a mortality game and those who live longer win that game. It seems logical that owning a longevity annuity would provide a great incentive to live a healthy lifestyle in retirement.

As you discuss deferred income annuities with your retirement base camp guide, be sure to learn about how these annuities work inside IRAs, and outside of IRAs. Ask about beneficiary features and only deal with highly rated insurance companies.

A close cousin to deferred income annuities are immediate income annuities. Immediate income annuities are the simplest kind of annuities to understand. A client writes a single check to an insurance company in exchange for a guaranteed monthly income for a defined period of time—usually for the entire life of one person or two. The older one is when purchasing an immediate income annuity, the higher the monthly payments will be into your bank account. As with deferred income annuities, be sure to ask about and understand the beneficiary features prior to making your purchase.

A feature that can be added to income annuities is an inflation rider. Any time you hear the word "rider" in the insurance world, just think of the words, "additional features." Additional features in life usually cost more. The way inflation riders work with income annuities is that the initial income back to you will be lower, then every year your income will be increased by a preset percentage.

Prior to retirement, be sure to check with your employer to see if they offer income annuities that you can purchase with some of your retirement plan dollars. Here in Washington State, those who have participated in the public employees Plan 3 have a fantastic option, called the Total Allocation Portfolio (TAP) Annuity. I'm not sure how many more years the TAP annuity will be offered but right now it's the best income annuity I've ever seen.

The payouts are relatively high at normal retirement ages and the TAP has a built in 3% annual inflation increase.

The funding for the TAP comes from the investment side of Plan 3. That's the side of Plan 3 that is similar to a 401(k). If you are a Washington state public employee participating in Plan 3, make sure your retirement base camp guide covers your options for the TAP annuity. If your advisor doesn't want to educate you about the TAP annuity—since he or she cannot be compensated from your purchase of the TAP—it's time for you to find a new advisor.

Later in this book I will teach you how all of these tools can come together to cover your retirement needs. For now, understand that annuities are one of the only mathematical certainties you can deploy. Annuities receive a lot of bad press.

When I hear someone talking down about annuities, I ask a very simple question: What else can I buy that will provide guaranteed lifetime income?

Annuities come in many varieties. Annuities date back to the Roman Empire where, "annua" mortality tables were established. Lump sums were exchanged for annual lifetime payments. The longer one lived, the more they emerged on the winning side of the equation. You'll often find references to annuity payments in historical novels and historical fiction. Interesting to note, the recipients of these lifetime payments often outlived their peers.

Annuities have played important roles in world history. For example, The National Pension Program for Soldiers was initiated in 1776 and provided income payments for soldiers and widows during the birth of our nation. In 1986 Congress passed tax reforms that made annuities one of the few financial instruments where people can invest unlimited amounts of money and receive tax deferral.

Modern annuities come in quite the variety pack. In addition to the immediate and deferred income annuities previously discussed, there are deferred annuities that are designed to provide potential growth along with available income features. Common varieties of deferred products include fixed annuities, variable annuities and index annuities.

A fixed annuity has characteristics similar to bank CDs. An investor puts aside money for a pre-determined number of years and receives a fixed interest rate. Usually the issuing insurance company sweetens the deal by offering a higher rate for the first year or so, then the rate settles to some lower guaranteed level. Fixed annuities don't charge fees, but there are surrender charges if the money is taken out prior to an agreed number of years—usually 5 or more. The income generated is tax deferred as long as it stays within an annuity. As the income gains are taken out, they are taxed.

Variable annuities combine the potential for investment growth with tax deferral and, quite often, are purchased with the addition of an income rider, a death benefit rider, or a combination of the two riders.

Let's revisit Joe and Mary, change their circumstances a little, and see how a variable annuity would work. Let's have Joe and Mary retiring in 3 years instead of 10. They still come to their retirement base camp with $500,000 but they no longer have the ability to weather market downturns, nor do they have 10 years to harvest mutual fund gains to put into deferred income annuities.

Joe and Mary invest their $500,000 into a variable annuity with a 5% guaranteed income rider. The money gets invested into sub accounts (similar to mutual funds) and is positioned for growth. After the first year, the insurance company will look at two numbers and whichever of those two numbers is higher will lock in as Joe and Mary's guaranteed income base. The insurance company will look at the net returns of the sub accounts and will compare that number to 5% of $500,000. For this illustration, let's say the funds increased by 10%, or $50,000. The income base is now $550,000 and the whole annual process starts over again. The next year the sub accounts do not increase by more than 5%, so the income base goes up by 5% of the previously locked in $550,000 so it is now $577,500. During the third year the investment sub accounts go down in value. Even during a down year, the income base increases by the guaranteed amount. So 5% more compounding on top of the $577,500 brings their income base to $606,375.

Now they are ready to retire and begin receiving their guaranteed lifetime income. Joe and Mary turn on their income stream and begin receiving 5% of the $606,375, or $2,500 per month. As long as they don't take out more than their annual guarantee, they will continue to receive those income payments for life, even if the actual investment value eventually goes to zero.

Notice that the 10-year strategy and the 3-year strategy have some similarities. Each strategy has plusses and minuses. In the 3-year strategy, Joe and Mary are in what Prudential has termed the retirement red zone. That's their term for the five years just before and the five years just after retirement. It's during that time when a severe market downturn can have the biggest disruption to a retirement portfolio.

The variable annuity comes with a 5% guaranteed payout while the mutual fund withdrawals are not guaranteed and the 4% withdrawal rate is only a suggested maximum.

Variable annuities generally don't have any sales charge to get in, but they are a more expensive option than mutual funds.

The variable annuities have annual mortality and expense charges, the rider has a charge and the sub accounts have management fees. Variable annuities usually have a surrender schedule as well. Investors can be charged if the money is removed during a set period of years—usually around 8. There are no surrender charges associated with taking one's normal income.

More expensive is not always a bad thing. Expenses that add value are often good for your retirement peace of mind. Think about driving your car on a twisty mountain road. If the car is your investment vehicle (stock funds), that car will perform the same way regardless of whether or not there are guard rails on the road. It will achieve the same speeds, steer the same, brake the same, and experience any negative occurrences like flat ties or overheating. Now close your eyes and imagine driving a mountain road with no guard rails between you and the thousand-foot drop off on the right. My palms sweat just thinking about it. I doubt that would be a well-traveled road.

Index annuities have fewer moving parts than variable annuities, and generally only charge a fee if an income rider is added. Index annuities also have surrender fees for early withdrawals.

Index annuities promise the investor a participation rate. In other words, the investor can participate in the upside of the stock market each year. If a person invested $100,000 with a 7% cap rate tied to the S&P 500 (A broad stock market index) here is what would happen after one year. If the S&P 500 increased by 10%, the index annuity would grow to $107,000 because the investor is capped at the 7% participation rate. Why would someone do that? Well, the answer lies in what happens if the S&P 500 goes down by 10%...or even more. If the S&P 500 drops during that year, the index annuity does not lose any value. It stays at $100,000.

Index annuities can go up in value. Index annuities cannot go down in value, and—for an extra charge—the annuity owner can add an income guarantee similar to the riders available on variable annuities.

Annuities of all sorts are tools to consider. There is no one perfect solution and most people at retirement base camp will be wise to allocate only some assets to annuities. Later I will cover a strategy to help you determine how much of your nest egg to place in guaranteed income products.

"Roger," I can hear many of you saying, "These annuity instruments don't sound bad. They actually have many attractive features. Why is it that I see ads all the time that say bad things about annuities?"

There are investment advisory firms out there that aggressively advertises against annuities. Those firms are marketing for you to place your investment money with them. They are selling their services. They do not have a corner on the truth. I have no reason to believe they do anything less than honorable with client money, but I do have a problem with any base camp guide who removes a whole set of tools from the toolbox. Would you head up Mt. Everest with a Sherpa who said, "I am the best climbing Sherpa in the world. I am so good at helping you climb that we do not need to bring any downside protection. No pick axe, no safety ropes, I only focus on going up." You going to entrust your hike up to 29,000 feet with that guide? I once thought this analogy to be pretty far out there until I read, *Into Thin Air,* by Jon Krakauer. He tells a side story of just such a reckless Sherpa. It did not end well.

Let me clarify what might seem like a couple of contradictory things I've written about. First, I wrote about stocks as investments and how they can be your friends and every investor should own some stocks. Then I talked about the dangers of stock market declines and why it's important to have some money that is protected by annuities. Both things can be true. When I talk about owning stocks, I mean just that…owning them. Not short-term speculation, not day trading, not trying to time the market. Stocks, in whatever form you own them, should be held as long-term assets that grow and pay dividends. Any United States historical look over 10, 15 and 20-year periods of time prove out that quality stocks increase in value over time. But, from time to time, stock markets can and will decline and sometimes those declines are fairly steep. So, for your necessary income during retirement, your plan should include guaranteed income that one can only get through annuities.

So why not put everything into annuities? Without any stocks in your portfolio, unless you have other assets—like rental properties—that can rise in value over time, you are likely to be on a fixed income. A fixed income simply means you are fixed into buying fewer things/experiences this year than last. Not an ideal place to be in an inflationary world.

As in mountain climbing, during retirement unexpected things can happen. A solid retirement plan will make preparations for the unforeseen. I call these events the "what ifs" in life. Through the course of life, you've prepared for many what ifs by owning home and auto insurance, health insurance, and hopefully life and disability insurance as well.

Being Prepared for the What Ifs that Life Can Toss Our Way

Life insurance can still play an important role in your retirement years, but another what if that needs to be talked about with your base camp guide is what to do if the day ever comes when you cannot take care of yourself. This can be an uncomfortable discussion to have. If you prefer to skip this section because you don't want to have that conversation, I'd ask you to have the conversation for the sake of your loved ones who would be the ones your physical and financial care would fall to if you ever needed living assistance.

In the world of long term care insurance there are six activities of daily living that insurance companies use to determine when a covered person qualifies for their insurance benefits to kick in. These activities of daily living (ADLs) are:

1. Bathing. The ability to clean oneself, brush teeth, shave, etc.
2. Dressing. The ability to dress oneself without struggling with buttons and zippers. (I think I have this one now based on the noises I make when trying to tie my own shoes.)
3. Eating. The ability to feed oneself.

4. Transferring. The ability to move around the house. Being able to get in and out bed.
5. Toileting. The ability to get on and off the toilet.
6. Countenance. The close cousin to number 5.

Most Long Term Care (LTC) policies are triggered when a person can no longer do two of the six ADLs. Yeah, I know, this is a most unpleasant discussion to have. Think about LTC insurance as asset protection. A long term care event without having Long Term Care Insurance is one thing that can come along in retirement and blow a huge hole in everything you've worked for. Needing long term care assistance is a giant storm that can approach out of nowhere on your mountain trek and, if you are not prepared with the proper tools from basecamp, it can send your household into financial ruin.

What tools should you acquire at basecamp?

Let's first take a look at traditional LTC policies then we will explore an emerging trend that—for many—offers a more attractive approach.

Traditional LTC policies are an agreement between the policyholder (you) and an insurance company. You pay annual premiums while the insurance company agrees to pay a certain amount of your care expenses when you can no longer perform the ADLs as previously described.

When buying LTC insurance, you are essentially buying a bucket of money. That bucket of money has some key points to understand. The first is called a daily benefit. For illustrative purposes, say you are buying a $200 daily benefit.

Second, you pick a length of coverage. How long will the insurance company pay you $200 per day if needed? If you picked a 3-year plan with a daily benefit of $200, you would have an initial bucket of LTC insurance of $219,000.

The third component of this coverage is similar to the deductible on your car or home insurance. In the LTC world, that deductible is referred to as the elimination period. If your policy has a 90-day elimination period, the LTC coverage would kick in after 90 days of you paying your own way after triggering the ADLs. 90 days seems to be a pretty standard elimination period. Shorter elimination periods, such as 30 days, are available but can drive premiums much higher.

The forth major component of LTC coverage is inflation protection. This is added as a rider on most policies. If you added a 5% compounded inflation rider to the $200 daily benefit, after one year of owning the policy your daily benefit would now be $210. The following year it would be $220.50, and *so it goes*... (I knew I could get a tribute to Kurt Vonnegut into my first book.)

LTC policies contain a myriad of riders and combinations of riders. Your base camp guide should be able to describe those riders in detail and help you understand which ones might be important on your journey.

One of the interesting reasons to consider traditional LTC insurance is what's called State Partnerships.

To understand state partnerships, one must first know a little bit about Medicaid. Medicaid is the state based program to provide long term care for people who can no longer pay their own care expenses. In order for a person to receive Medicaid based care, one must spend their assets down to almost nothing and then the state caps the amount of income one can have. The current numbers for your state can be located through a quick web search.

Let's just take a look at a rough outline for a married couple who live in Washington state. My purpose here is not to cover Medicaid in detail. You should talk to a Medicaid specialist or research the subject on your own if you want to learn more. I am simply putting forth a basic understanding of one aspect of Medicaid in order to help you understand what role the state partnership component of LTC coverage can play in protecting assets.

If Bret and Tammy have $300,000 of assets and Tammy needs long-term care, the state would make them spend their assets down to $123,600 (2018 rules) before Medicaid would kick in.

Now, let's circle back to traditional LTC insurance that qualifies as a state partnership plan. If Tammy had LTC insurance of $300,000 (her bucket of money), the picture would change dramatically. First, Tammy would not be going to the state for help. She'd be covered by her own LTC protection. But say a very devastating prolonged illness, such as Alzheimer's, came along and Tammy spent her LTC bucket of money down to zero. Now, she is forced to get Medicaid help for her care. Because she had a LTC policy in a state partnership plan, her new Medicaid spenddown number is no longer $123,600…it is $300,000. Basically, the state is willing to reward people who take personal responsibility. (Governments rewarding personal responsibility…I hope I didn't trigger any heart attacks out there with those crazy words.)

One more rider to touch on, then on to alternatives to traditional LTC insurance. Shared Care is an important rider to consider. With Shared Care, each spouse would have access to the other's bucket of money if one bucket runs dry. With Bret and Tammy, it would look like this. If Bret and Tammy had LTC coverage and they elected the Shared Care rider, Tammy's bucket goes to zero, then she could continue receiving benefits by accessing Bret's bucket. (Some insurance companies actually create a 3rd bucket when Shared Care is elected, thereby allowing for Tammy to access 3 additional years while Bret's bucket remains intact.)

On your retirement journey, I wish you nothing but bright days and a healthy life. But don't be afraid to swallow your pride and admit that none of us are invincible. Take care of this both for your own future dignity and for the financial protection of your loved ones.

You and your base camp guide(s) might decide that an alternative to traditional LTC insurance is a better fit for your journey.

To understand the genesis of Long Term Care hybrid products it helps to examine the good and bad parts of the traditional LTC policies previously described.

The good parts of those policies are 1. They offer state partnerships, 2. The inflation protection is an important rider, 3. Shared Care can offer protection against a prolonged illness of one spouse. 4. They are simple to understand, and 5. For what you are protecting (everything you own) they offer a pretty good value for the price.

What do people dislike about traditional LTC policies? 1. The premiums (what you pay) go on forever, until such time as you qualify to receive benefits. 2. The insurance company can raise the premiums anytime. They can't raise rates specifically on just you, but they can—and do—file for across-the-board rate increases from time to time. Think about a policy taken out when you are 60. If rates get raised 4-5 times between then and when you turn 85 and need the policy, it can be very taxing on one's retirement income. When they raise the rates, the insurance companies usually offer you the option of reducing your benefits instead of taking the rate increase. Tough choices as we age and notice our health declining. 3. If you never use the insurance, there is not any death benefit to your heirs. All those years of paying premiums were for something never used. (There are riders that offer some death benefits. Remember, though, each added rider equals higher premiums.)

Those are the three biggest complaints I've encountered over the years when it comes to traditional LTC insurance.

Enter hybrids. Hybrids are LTC coverage built on the framework of life insurance policies. Hybrids check all three boxes on the negative side: 1. There is a finite amount of money you pay in, then you are finished. 2. The rates cannot be raised on you. What you and the insurance company agreed to at the beginning is what you are obligated to pay, and that's all. 3. The hybrid policies have a death benefit, so if you never use the LTC money, your heirs will receive a death benefit. The hybrid policies usually also have some sort of cash refund too, but that's rarely used since people buy these things to protect against needing long term care assistance and once they buy the policy, they rarely change their minds.

Many hybrids do offer inflation protection. They are generally for one person, so shared care is not part of that equation right now. Some companies have invented creative work arounds to mirror shared care and those solutions will evolve as the market changes to meet the needs of consumers.

Hybrids are not state partnership qualified at this time because they are life insurance vehicles.

Speaking with a professional base camp guide about all your options is the best course of action. If your primary guide/advisor is not well versed in LTC options, bring in a specialist who does know the subject. This is too important to leave to guess work and amateur hour.

Time for one final what if tool then I'll bring this all together.

Before you read another word, get yourself to YouTube and type in, "Alan King, Survived by His Wife." The top two results will be Mr. King doing a stand up routine, and an interview from 1988 on the David Letterman show. Either—or both—will do for your watching pleasure. I can promise this: You will laugh about obituaries.

www.youtube.com/watch?v=83yyMAdbrpE&feature=player_embedded

I'll pause this book while you go watch Alan King…

How was that for easing into the subject of death through humor?

Looks like we can safely move forward under the premise of women living longer than men. The very first life insurance joke I ever heard goes like this: A woman comes home and proudly announces to her husband that she has taken out life insurance on both of them. "That way," she explains, "When one of us dies, I'll be able to travel to Paris."

The final tool for a successful retirement is life insurance. Life insurance can, perhaps, be your most important tool of all. A well-constructed life insurance plan can provide income protection that is not connected to the stock market, it can help you reduce exposure to taxes, it can cover your long term care risk, it can secure your legacy, and it can provide blessings to your loved ones long after you are gone. A good life insurance plan is akin to a Swiss Army Knife. You can load in many blades and use them as needed.

A word about Term Life Insurance. Term Insurance can be a tremendously powerful tool when people are young, raising families and building assets. It's a way to trade little dollars for large amounts of death benefit. Term insurance is simple to understand. You pay an insurance company a fixed amount of money in exchange for a death benefit that is guaranteed to stay in place for a certain number of years, e.g., 10, 20, or 30.

While term life insurance might belong in the portfolios of the young, term life insurance has very little place in a retirement plan. Think about this: What is the only life insurance that truly matters? It's the policy that is in force on the day you die. Term does not—cannot—guarantee that it will be in force on the day you die. Eventually you get so old that insurance companies stop offering legitimate (large death benefit) term policies.

At your retirement base camp, you should have a serious conversation about the benefits of Whole Life Insurance. In fact, if we say the average person checking in to retirement base camp is 55, ideally, the conversation and getting started with Whole Life should have already taken place 10-15 years earlier.

However, if that is not the case for you, just remember, the best time to have planted an oak tree in your back yard would have been twenty years ago. The next best time would be today rather than tomorrow.

Often, when the conversation of Whole Life comes up, people have a tendency to think, or say, "Well, isn't that more expensive than Term Insurance?" In terms of money going into the policy, yes, Whole Life is more expensive. But when you consider the value it brings to your overall retirement plan, I can say that a good Whole Life policy is worth every dollar you put into it, and more.

Should you put some money into an investment account that is not subjected to the downswings of the stock market? Should you put some money into an account that grows tax-deferred and can be accessed mostly tax-free? Should you put some money into a long-term care protection plan? Should you put some money into a life insurance policy to take care of your spouse if your part of the income equation goes to zero? Do you want to leave a legacy to any charities? Do you want any family members to remember that you individually cared about them enough to bless them? A good Whole Life policy can do all of the above in one awesome package.

For my way of thinking as a retirement planning guide, Whole Life Insurance took on new attractiveness when the long-term care riders started to be added several years ago. This is different from the hybrid LTC products. Whole Life is primarily a life insurance policy designed to give you a significant death benefit that will be in place on the day you die. The "what if" of potentially needing long term care is added to the policy as a rider. So, let's say you have a $500,000 death benefit on your Whole Life policy. By adding the LTC rider, you would be able to access most of your death benefit to pay monthly long term care expenses over a certain number of months, or years. Doing so will, of course, lower your death benefit over time because you are accessing the death benefit money while you are still alive.

If you have previously purchased a Whole Life policy, or any other kind of cash value policy, and you do not have an LTC access rider, I'd suggest having a conversation with an experienced life insurance representative and see if moving to a new policy might be in your best interest.

The purpose of this book is not to teach you every single detail about life insurance. I want you to know enough to seek advice and see how that advice can improve your chances for a successful retirement trek.

Putting it All Together

In the previous pages we've touched on ascension gear, downside protection, and being prepared for the what ifs. In every single retirement plan I've been involved with, a central question comes up: Will I have enough money to retire and how do I know when I have enough money?

Take a look at the single page Retirement Base Camp planning I use when first introducing clients to this concept. Using these three planning buckets brings all the previous information together and will help you answer—with your guide—some key questions about your retirement readiness.

First, a tip of the hat to financial author, Tom Hegna, who's book, Pay Checks and Play Checks provided me with impactful language to express this concept. Tom has written many retirement planning books and he travels the country teaching solid principles of successful retirement. Prior to hearing Tom, I referred to these retirement categories as the Essentials, Enjoyment, and Legacy Buckets. I liked Tom's terminology much better, so, with his gracious permission, I now call these buckets Pay Checks, Play Checks, and Philanthropy Checks. I highly recommend Tom Hegna's books for those who want to continue learning about success in retirement.

*Date*_____

Retirement Base Camp Planning for _____

Pay Checks*	Play Checks*	Philanthropy Checks
Goals:	Goals:	While Living:
		Final Checks:
Resources:	Resources:	Resources:

The What Ifs:

Action steps for you:

Action steps for Roger's team:

*Credit to Tom Hegna

With this page, a conversation can be facilitated with you and your advisor. I'd also submit that good advisors help facilitate conversations between married couples that otherwise may never take place. We get involved and we ask questions. We patiently listen, then ask follow-up questions. Many people never take the time to have a marriage sit down and really discuss retirement hopes, dreams and fears. Many couples have no idea if or when they can retire. Many don't even know how their spouse would fill in the Play Checks bucket.

When retirement does arrive, suddenly every day is a Saturday and people often want to re-invent themselves. Why? Because now they have the time to live life differently. Time to travel. Time to take up hobbies. Time to volunteer.

The first bucket, Pay Checks, is the most boring bucket, but it's also the most essential to get right. For every hundred people reading this book, the Pay Checks bucket would be filled with similar items. The basics of life go in here. Housing, taxes, utilities, food, auto fuel and maintenance, insurances, phones, etc. Be sure to take a thorough inventory of your essential needs. Your retirement planning guide can provide you with worksheets to help make sure you don't forget anything. Things like garbage service and lawn care might get overlooked without a detailed checklist.

Once you know everything that goes into that fist bucket, you need to put a monthly price tag on that bucket. Does it take $3,000 to make your basic world go 'round, or does it take $7,000? Numbers will vary widely depending on lifestyles. You must know your accurate number.

Next, under resources, begin to list your income sources that come with secure or guaranteed money—only list secure sources. We'll get to things like stocks and mutual funds in a bit. For now, only list Pensions, Social Security, Annuities and other secure income items. Add those income sources together and compare that number to the expenses in that same bucket. Is there a surplus? Is there a gap?

If you have a surplus, congratulations but hold the celebration. If you need $5,000 per month for your essentials, and you have $5,700 of monthly secure income, over time, inflation will cause that $5,000 figure to increase. So, there will come a day when you might have a gap instead of a surplus and it is important to plan ahead for that eventuality.

Most people will have an immediate gap to deal with, let alone a future gap based on increasing prices. The first step in dealing with any problem in life is to know the truth of the problem.

If you have a $1,000 gap, that means you need to look at your other resources, (i.e. mutual funds), and calculate how much money you will need to carve out to provide that extra $1,000 per month. Like the scenario above where those people have a surplus, you too will need to plan ahead for inflation.

The very minimum standard for your first bucket is to generate enough guaranteed income so as to never experience a pay cut. A far better approach is to design your Pay Checks Bucket to never experience a pay cut, AND build in future income increases.

Can you begin to see why some of those income annuity strategies can play such an important role in your retirement future?

By partnering with a wise financial planner to help you here, that planner will look at all your income sources and assess the risks associated with each source. For example, a married couple will likely be calculating two social security figures to contribute to the Pay Checks equation. When one spouse dies, all the numbers will change. Here again is another endorsement for life insurance. Whole Life can help fill the hole left from a death.

I'll touch more on inflation protection for the Pay Checks bucket in a bit, as that topic relates to the Play Checks bucket.

Before we move on to the Play Checks bucket, it's a good idea to create a bucket within a bucket back in the Pay Checks area. That bucket within a bucket is where you might isolate a certain amount of money to generate the income needed to pay for life insurance and long term care protection. For example, if the premiums to cover those items cost $15,000 per year, and you can get a guaranteed income of 5%, you'd need to set aside $300,000 into that guaranteed investment product to put your life insurance and long term care coverages on auto pilot.

To me, the most rewarding part of being a financial planner is working with people to fill in the Play Checks bucket. Face it, for most of our lives we trade time for money. Hopefully you've been wise and have set aside money and invested over time. Now, you are at retirement base camp and you are deciding what you want to do when you get to keep more of your time. Will you travel, take up hobbies, volunteer, spend time with the grandchildren? Play Checks literally represents a spendable bucket to finance your bucket list. What to do when every day is now your Saturday!

This is the bucket where your investments in stocks, mutual funds and ETFs belong. Your money here should be positioned to grow by more than you need, or want, to spend. Take a couple who has $500,000 to invest for their Play Checks bucket. They have $30,000 worth of annual fun goals and the market delivers a 15% return one year. Their $500,000 is now $575,000. If they were to take $30,000 from the gains and stash that in their bank, guess what is paid for? Yep, their fun list for the year.

Now you're relaxing on a beach when the couple next to you starts freaking out because the stock market is crashing. You order another round and continue relaxing.

Remember when I said we'd circle back and talk about inflation protection for the Pay Checks bucket? This couple who just harvested $30,000 from $75,000 in gains has $45,000 in gains that can be deployed to improve their future against the tides of inflation. Perhaps a deferred income annuity would make sense here. They still have their $500,000 invested for future fun money, they have their fun money for this year and now they've stashed away a future pay raise. It's amazing what doing something like that a few times early in retirement can do for you later in retirement.

Harvesting money to split between play checks and bolstering paychecks will not happen every year. In years when investments returns are small, or even negative, perhaps its more camping and fewer all-inclusive resorts.

Important Note: The impact of taxes aren't being ignored here. Various types of accounts have different tax treatments, so always check with your tax professional before moving money. For illustrative purposes I've only discussed gross figures.

The Philanthropy Bucket is a place for you to dream a little. Where do you fall on this continuum of leaving a financial legacy?

←—————————————————————————→

Whatever   Maximum
Is Left   Impact

There are organizations in your community that do tremendous work with causes that you probably care about. Something as simple as naming a charity as a partial beneficiary on your life insurance, or in your Will, can improve the lives of those still here when you are gone.

If you find yourself over on the right side of this continuum, I highly recommend sharing your heart with a good estate planning attorney because there are tremendous planning tools available that can help you truly deliver maximum impact through your legacy.

A client of mine, Jerry, recently addressed the board of his church. He asked them, "What is the greatest financial asset of this church?" After a few members proffered answers such as the land and buildings, Jerry gave his answer: "It's us old people." Jerry and I have set up tools for him to give regularly in his living years and he has his church built into his will. If more people would talk to their financial advisors and attorneys about giving, I believe many charities across our land would be able to spend less time worrying about money and more time helping people and animals.

Many retirees are combining the Enjoyment Bucket with the Philanthropy Bucket. They are not waiting until the end of the road to make a difference. Travel plans? Search out a nearby orphanage or other charity that would benefit from some volunteer time and a generous donation. Your travels will take on more meaning and you will be changing lives for the better.

Another of my clients, Heather, has actually traveled to Nepal and has hiked to the real Base Camp. Along the way, she spent some time volunteering at an orphanage. Heather described how the leader of that orphanage can make 200 American Dollars last an entire month in feeding a dozen or more children. Most of us can scratch that check and never miss it from our bank. Yet look at the many lives impacted. Consider adding charity to your adventures.

There are so many boxes to check at your personal retirement basecamp. Make sure the guide(s) you hire are comprehensive and they have a system to assure you cover as many gaps as possible.

Advice [n]: *guidance or recommendations concerning prudent future action, typically given by someone regarded as knowledgeable or authoritative.*

Over the past several months I've had the pleasure of sitting down with nine professionals in various lines of work to interview them for the next chapters of my advice-driven book. Each of these people has participated voluntarily and I personally have learned a great deal while going through these Q&A sessions. I hope you enjoy the interviews and, please, if some of these people speak to areas in your life where you could use some guidance, get in touch with them.

TABLE OF CONTENTS

DEDICATION v

INTRODUCTION vii

CASE STUDY ix

Chapter 1: Brian Gracyalny & Shelley Autrey 1

Chapter 2: Hugh Himmelreich. 23

Chapter 3: Tim Brummett 43

Chapter 4: Korrin Fotheringham 59

Chapter 5: Megaen Paladin-Childress 73

Chapter 6: Julie Adams 91

Chapter 7: Hanna & Greg Stewart-Longhurst 109

Chapter 8: Ken Bohenek 125

Chapter 9: Diane Gardener 147

CLOSING THOUGHTS 163

Chapter 1
BRIAN GRACYALNY & SHELLEY AUTREY

Brian Gracyalny and Shelley Autrey are with All Medicare Solutions in Spokane Valley, WA, an independent insurance agency whose primary focus is Medicare. The agency serves clients in the entire Pacific Northwest, as well as California, Arizona, Utah and Wisconsin.

Brian Gracyalny is the owner of All Medicare Solutions. He's been in the insurance business since 1980. In 1997, he started his own independent financial planning agency, Freedom Financial Group, and founded All Medicare Solutions in 2008.

The agency's goal is to provide individualized and affordable solutions for its clients.

Brian is also an Air Force Veteran who served for nearly 10 years.

Shelley Autrey has held various sales positions for more than 30 years. She began Medicare insurance sales in 2009, and joined All Medicare Solutions in 2010.

Shelley believes her greatest asset is her

ability to convey genuine concern for her clients, which lets them openly discuss their situations with her.

Roger: Brian Gracyalny, and Shelley Autrey are with All Medicare Solutions in Spokane.

I'm excited about this interview, specifically because as a financial planner, a question that comes up with my clients, which comes up for every American citizen as they're approaching the age of 65, is, "What do we do about this age-required change in healthcare, for Medicare and things like that?" That question used to scare me to death. But then I met Shelley, who I found to be very knowledgeable. So I was able to tell people, "Contact Shelley, she'll help you out."

So why don't you both tell me a little bit about yourselves? Brian, how did you start All Medicare Solutions, and what got you into this field?

Brian: Actually Roger, I was doing primarily what you're doing, financial planning. I began working for a captive agency insurance company called The Independent Order of Foresters in 1980. In 1987, they started a wholly-owned subsidiary called Foresters Equity Services. Through that, we were able to offer mutual funds and variable products. I stayed with them until 1997, when I went out and became independent. I continued primarily doing financial planning. I was doing very little in the way of just straight life insurance. It was really a more comprehensive approach. So I did that independently until 2005, at which time Medicare came out with a prescription drug plan and many of my clients who had grown old with me, began asking about how to pick the right one. At the time, there were 56 different prescription drug plans available here in Spokane. So I started doing some research.

But I had no intention of getting involved with Medicare. To me it was a foreign concept, kind of like it is for you. There's so much involved with this. But as I did more checking and research, I actually enrolled about half a dozen of my clients into a plan on the Medicare website. That first year, Humana had four different prescription drug plans, and one of those four was probably the correct plan for 95% of the population in the United States that first year. I ended up getting appointed with Humana, and everything just totally changed. I don't do financial planning anymore. I deal exclusively with Medicare. I started All Medicare Solutions in 2008. I now have about 15 agents, and 95% of what we do is related exclusively to Medicare, Social Security, The Advantage Plans, Supplements, and Prescription Drug Plans. We've basically become experts in the Medicare business.

Roger: Shelley, how about you? When did you join up with them? You had had some background in understanding medical plans prior to that, right?

Shelley: I started working with All Medicare Solutions in 2010. I had done some long-term care in the late-90s in Seattle. But I'm from Spokane, and decided to move back here.

Roger: So people come to you around the age of 65 and they're entering this very confusing world of Medicare. What's your process? What do you do with them when they come to you and say, "Help me navigate this"?

Shelley: We start with getting a list their prescription drugs and their doctors. Depending on the client, we ask questions about income to see if they get extra help. Then we do what's called a drug run on the Medicare website. From there, we set up the appointment and go through all the different plans and choices, showing them where their drugs will be covered at the best cost, and what their doctors will take. And answer any questions. To me, it's a simple process. To clients, it's not a simple process.

Roger: What are some of the dangers of people trying to do it themselves?

Shelley: They will pick a plan under which their drugs aren't covered, or that doesn't cover their doctor. That would be bad, because they could pay a lot of money for some prescriptions. Take insulin for example. Mine costs around $500 a month. So, if insulin is not on their formulary, that's a lot of money. And they can't change plans until the next fall, and then that plan is not active until January.

Roger: So, that leads into an important question. As people are reading this book and they see their age in here, when should they contact you?

Shelley: About three months prior to their 65th birthday month.

Roger: So it has nothing to do with any type of open enrollment at the end of the year?

Shelley: Open enrollment doesn't affect them until they're already in Medicare. Then, that's October 15th through December 7th, every fall.

Brian: I'd like to add, we have a discussion with our younger clients about whether or not they should retire at 65. Because the options are different if they're going to continue to be gainfully employed, and if they have health insurance through their employer. We then evaluate their situation, what their part of the cost is for their health insurance, and we can quite simply assist them in determining whether they're better off financially to sign up for Medicare. They can decide if they want to come off their group plan, or whether they're better to stay on their group plan, until they actually are going to retire.

For most people, it's still a confusing process. Some people tell them they have to sign up for Part B whether they want to or not. Some say they don't have to. We answer all of those types of questions. And again, it depends on their situation, even the size of the employer, whether Medicare pays first or whether the employer pays first. There are a lot of moving parts, and it's different for everyone.

Shelley was talking about the prescriptions and the mistakes someone can make trying to do it on their own. Someone doing it on their own is going to select whatever pharmacy they go to. There is a huge difference in cost with most of the plans, and it's specifically due to which pharmacy you use. Because there are preferred pharmacies and there are standard pharmacies. We have two pharmacies in Spokane County that cover all the plans that are available. But most people are just going to put in whatever pharmacy they go to, and they literally could be costing themselves hundreds and sometimes thousands of dollars a year. Most people are willing to change their pharmacy if it's going to save them that much money.

Roger: That is actually one of the reasons I'm so excited about this interview, because I think it's an important public service.

Brian, I love your story about moving from financial planning to Medicare. Because I look at all the things I have to know in financial planning, and I don't want to try to become an expert in this area. But to be able to partner and say, "Hey, here's somebody that can help you with that." When people come to you and go through that process, it must be a real relief when they come out the other side. Without naming names, can you tell any stories of people who came in full of apprehension or confusion, and went out your door feeling like the sun could once again shine on them?

Brian: There are lots of stories. We even help them apply for Medicare. And everything we do is at no cost to them. We're paid by the insurance company. It's really a no-brainer process, because Medicare controls the commissions we're paid on the products that we sell. And we get paid the same amount regardless of what company they go with. So, for the client, it at least should be comforting to know I'm not trying to sell this particular company because I make more money. We get paid the same thing regardless of what company they go with.

Medicare made a change about six years ago that a lot of agents complained about, because it was kind of a free-for-all before then. But it's actually a very good system, and it really does help protect the consumer from someone just trying to sell whatever is paying them the most commission. In this case, there is no difference.

Shelley: Brian has a story about clients from up north, and it always brings tears to his eyes. But this is a very good example of what he can do.

Brian: I have a client up in Newport, who wanted to know if I could help her friend, who lived in Idaho. This was during the annual enrollment period. Her friend was 66. When she turned 65 the year before, she had no idea what to do. So she did nothing, except sign up for Medicare Part B. All she had was Medicare with no Supplement or Advantage plan, or prescription drug plan.

At the time, she didn't really have any health issues. But about six months later, she got this really weird disease that put her in the hospital for 10 days. Almost a year later, she was still receiving treatment for it. She was spending over $8,000 a year on her prescriptions, because she didn't have a prescription drug plan. She had spent tens of thousands of dollars for her share of the cost of the hospitalizations and the other medical work that she had to have done. She was paying 20% of that. And she was going through her nest egg, her 401(k) and her IRAs.

So I got a list of all her prescriptions and all her doctors, and I put her into a plan. And when everything was said and done, she was going to pay no more than $354 a year for her prescriptions, instead of $8,000 a year.

And the three of us just sat there and cried like babies. Because it changed her life. She had her retirement back. And she still is very happy and very appreciative of the help we gave her. Because she qualified for some pharmacy assistance programs that she didn't know anything about. And we got some of her prescriptions from Canada, which saved her a ton of money.

Roger: Wow. Bless you. That's doing the work of angels.

Brian: I just ran across an email I got from one of my clients. Three years ago, she called our office on the last day of the annual enrollment period. She had been up literally the entire night before talking to Medicare, trying to figure out which plan was going to cover her prescription. She was in her 70s and only took one prescription, a medication called Armor Thyroid, which no one covers. It's a natural medication, and it's not covered on the formulary by any of the companies.

She wanted to know whether there was any possibility we could see her, because it was the last day of the annual enrollment period. I was able to have one of our agents meet with her. She was paying around $90 a month for her Armor Thyroid. I found a discount card that got it down to $30 a month. She just started crying. She said, "You have no idea what $60 a month means to me." She sent me an email thanking me, and she called us her guardian angels. She said, "God sent me to you guys. He led me here today." Then about a week later, I found another card, one that was a little over $19 a month. I sent her an email with it attached, saying, "Guardian Angel, just checking in."

So that's what we do. We have alternatives to help people from going into what's called "the gap," or "the donut hole." We literally save our clients hundreds of thousands of dollars every year, because we're there to serve them. We could care less what company they sign up with. We just want to help them save as much money as possible for their specific situation. That's what my whole agency is about. That's why I do this.

Roger: That's fantastic. I can feel the genuine ethos of what you do. It's tremendous.

As we've talked, you've touched on some terms. I don't think we need to explain all of Medicare in this book, but would you give us a basic framework of the different parts?

Brian: Medicare consists of what they refer to in letters as Medicare Part A, Part B, Part C, and Part D. Anyone enrolling in Medicare automatically gets Part A. Part A takes care of hospital, skilled nursing, and hospice care. And there's no premium for that. That's paid through the 2.7% Medicare tax they were paying while they were working. So there's no cost for that. This year, there's about a $1,460 deductible for the first 60 days of a hospitalization. So that's all you would pay for the hospital itself, if you were hospitalized for less than 60 days.

Medicare Part B takes care of everything else. Doctor visits, lab work, diagnostic tests, therapy. Everything that's done outside the hospital is covered under Part B. You pay a premium of $134 a month for that.

That can change a little bit from year to year. And then you have a $183 deductible. So you have to pay the first $183 of Part B expenses. After that, Medicare pays 80%. You're responsible for 20% of the Medicare-approved amount, which is always less than the billed amount.

So that takes care of the medical part of this. As I just explained, 20% can add up to tens of thousands of dollars, as with the woman in Idaho. Then you have your prescription drug coverage, which is part D. Here in Spokane County, and in most counties, there are 20-30 different prescription drug plans to choose from. Some people will just pick a plan based on the premium or not having a deductible amount. But we're looking at the overall picture. We're looking for the best value for each individual client's situation. If they don't sign up for Part D, a prescription drug plan, when they're first eligible, then they will incur a penalty if they ever want to have a plan in the future. That penalty is one percent per month for each month that they did not have a plan. And it's one percent of the average national cost of all prescription drug plans in the entire country, which changes every year.

Roger: So, it's something that can be corrected, but it can cost some money for people to get back into that?

Brian: Correct. Take someone who was eligible for a prescription plan starting in 2005 but didn't sign up. If they want to start one now, their penalty is

	approximately $40-45 a month, on top of whatever the premium is.
Roger:	Okay, they're not writing a check to cover the last five or 10 years, they've added extra monthly cost going forward. That's interesting. I just learned something new, as will lots of people reading this.

So, I've got Parts A, B, and D. What's the elusive C? |
| Brian: | If you're doing a prescription drug plan, then you're normally going to do what's called a Medicare Supplement. The Medicare Supplements are all standardized, and they're lettered A through N. And the different plans are all standardized, so it doesn't matter what company it's with. An N is an N, an F is an F, etc. And Medicare is making a change in Plan F, which is currently considered the Cadillac of plans. Because, between Medicare and a Plan F Supplement, everything medical is covered, 100%. You have no out-of-pocket costs for medical. Now we always differentiate between prescription drug coverage and medical. They are two distinctly different things. So, they normally would have a supplement, and then some of the other supplements cover almost everything. The Plan G covers everything except the Part B deductible, which is $183. After that, everything's just like an F. They are all standardized. So again, all we do is look at who's got the lowest premium. |
| Roger: | So, is Part C what you add in? |

Brian: No, Part C is combining A, B, and D all into one plan, managed by a private insurance company. And the insurance company now takes care of paying for your prescriptions and your medical. Instead of you providing your doctor with a separate card for your Medicare and Medicare Supplement, and a separate card to your pharmacy for prescriptions, you have one card that you provide to your doctor and pharmacy. And everything is processed in one fell swoop by the private insurance company. And Medicare pays that insurance company a flat monthly amount for each client that's enrolled in their plan.

So for anyone that's a nerd like me, Medicare has what they call the "capitation rate." That's how much it costs Medicare per month, per Medicare beneficiary, and they do this in every county in the United States.

The capitation rate here in Spokane is a little over $1,000 a month. So it costs Medicare about $1,000 per month per Medicare beneficiary to provide them benefits. Medicare pays 90% of that capitation rate to the private insurance company. So they're saving 10%. And the insurance company is now taking the risk. And there's no medical underwriting, there's no qualification. The only thing that can prevent you from getting an Advantage Plan, a Part C Plan, is if you have end stage renal disease and you're on dialysis. Then you have to have Medicare and a supplement.

Roger: Boy, this is the first time in my life I've really understood all that stuff. So then the supplements are the next subject, correct?

Brian: The supplements complement A and B, and then you have a prescription drug plan on top of that.

Here in Washington, we have about 26 different companies that offer the Medicare supplements. And again, we're just looking at each individual person's situation to determine which plan is going to work best for them. Because the plans are standardized, but the premiums are not. There can be over $100 a month difference in monthly premium from one company to another for the exact same plan. It doesn't make a lot of sense, but that's the way it is.

Roger: So, the premiums can vary, but it sounds to me like the real value you bring is being able to figure out which company is the right fit for your client.

Brian: On prescription drug plans or advantage plans. We do the same thing for both. Shelley referred to it as the "drug run". We do that for both the prescription drug programs and the advantage plans, so we have everything we need to help the client make an informed decision based on their specific situation.

Roger: When I first reached out to Shelley about doing this interview, you were coming up on open enrollment. And you said, "Please, can we wait until after that?" So take me through open enrollment. What is that like? What's the pace of that? How many people are you seeing a day?

Shelley: I probably have about 800 to 900 clients, and I send cards out every fall. They call me starting October first. So, my phone rings nonstop for about two weeks, easy. I'd say we have six to eight appointments a day.

Brian: Yes, 45 to 50 appointments a week. For seven weeks.

Shelley: And it's seven days a week. The only day off I take is Thanksgiving. I'm there taking care of my clients. I'm also getting referrals from my clients. Because that's really how I work now: by referrals, and my existing base.

Roger: Walk me through the process. They've gone through and set up all their parts, they've got their supplements and everything. And open enrollment comes along.

Shelley: Now you can look at your drug plan and core Advantage plan. I review that with anyone that calls me. If they don't, everything stays the same and rolls over to the next year. However, a good majority like to have it reviewed.

Roger: And then they're sending their friends and neighbors to you. Because we're all going to be 65 someday. So, you sort of have clientele lined up.

Shelley: That's exactly right. They all say, "Gee, I don't know anybody. Oh, wait!" Sometimes I have whole families that come in. I'm not exaggerating.

Roger: Or as Brian alluded to, with me being a financial planner for 25 years, I'll sit down with people and we'll sigh, "We're getting old, it's time to call Shelley."

Shelley: Yes, it does happen. We can't stop that.

Roger: You said earlier, the open enrollment period is October 15 through December 7th. There's a lot of work to do in there. That's the intense part of it. The rest of the time meeting with clients, you're generally trying to get them a few months before their 65th birthday?

Shelley: Correct. And now, like I said, I just work off referrals this time of year. But after a while, there are only so many clients you can help in open enrollment. It gets a little overwhelming.

Roger: Brian, you said you have 15 agents?

Brian: Yes. In between all the appointments during the open enrollment period, we are still talking to dozens of people a day. Because it's very important for everyone on Medicare to understand, just because you were happy with your plan this year, doesn't mean you will be next year. Because the plans can change the formulary, they can add or drop prescriptions. They can quit taking the doctor you're seeing. There are moving parts with everything involved with Medicare, whether they're doing a supplement and a drug plan, or whether they're doing an Advantage plan.

We don't have to see all our clients every year, but we have to review. We have to at least talk with them to make sure that if there's anything that's changed, we still need to rerun everything through our system to make sure they're still going to be covered properly for the next year. Because they only have that seven-week window to make a change. And then, again, from January first to February 14th, they have the right to disenroll from their Advantage Plan and go back to original Medicare. But other than that, they're stuck in it for the rest of the year if there's something that didn't go right.

And we have about 6,000 clients in my office. We go through tons of paper and lots of drug runs. Again, we don't have to see all of those clients. But probably 40 to 50% of them are going to want to see us. Some of them just because they like Shelley and the other agents. They really do. A lot of these clients just become our friends. They sincerely appreciate what we do.

Roger: 10,000 baby boomers a day turn 65. And that's going to continue for a while. There are 1,000 a month just in Spokane County. It's going to be a booming business for the next 10 or 15 years.

Does your organization get contacted or interviewed by the media at all during open enrollment?

Shelley: No, but I keep telling Brian he needs to do that. He's the professional talker.

Brian: I am seriously considering talking to a radio station about doing a call-in show about Medicare and prescription drugs, and Medicare & Social Security.

Roger: I think that would be very beneficial, and you'd be very good at it. You have a way of articulating complex themes in plain English. I try to talk to people that same way. Once you start talking "financialese," then people just glaze over.

You touched on Social Security. How does that tie in with what you do, and the education pieces there?

Brian: I guess because of my financial planning background, I still see Social Security and Medicare as melded together, so we help them apply for Medicare, and we can help them apply for Social Security. All done on line and it's a very simple, fast process. It takes less than 10 minutes to apply for Medicare, and a little bit longer to apply for Social Security because there are a few more questions. But we assist our clients in doing that. If someone is under 65 and contacting us saying they want to apply for Social Security, then we have a serious conversation to help them understand that unless you have medical coverage through your employer, medical costs alone are going to be huge until you're eligible for Medicare.

Roger: When I'm dealing with people who want to retire early, that's always the number one subject.

I've learned so much in our conversation. Is there anything we haven't touched on that you deem as important to share?

Shelley: We help with all the facets. Depending on their income, we help our clients get extra help with Pharmacy Assistance programs. We help get their Part B premium paid for, if they need it.

Brian: We monitor over 200 Canadian pharmacies. Because in Canada, just as in the U.S., there's a big difference from one pharmacy to another. But the cost of prescriptions in Canada is substantially less than the cost of prescriptions here. And they don't have patent protection as long, so many drugs that are brand-name drugs here do have the true generic available in Canada.

We have new clients every year who are already getting something from Canada. We ask them which pharmacy they're using, and we give them the comparison. And usually they're paying anywhere from $20 to $40 more every month than what they could be getting it for. We do this for anybody. They don't have to be on Medicare. They can be under 65 and if they're having a problem with a prescription, we're just there to serve. So, we'll just tell them where to go, or we'll send them an email with a link to the website. It's not rocket science, it's just that we've done a lot of research in every avenue there is to try to save clients' money on their prescriptions, and on their medical.

When it comes to supplements, we monitor all 26 of these companies. Because, no one company is going to be the lowest cost forever. There will always be a company that will come in at a lower cost at some point in time. And Washington is a very consumer-friendly state when it comes to Medicare. Someone has the right to change from one Medicare supplement to another, either with the same company or with a different company, any time they want to. Not during the annual enrollment period, but they can change any time they want. So, we monitor the costs of those 26 companies, and we call our clients if their current company is now $225 a month for a Plan F, and another company is $200 a month. We're going to contact that client to see if they want to change. Because there's no underwriting. It's guaranteed issue.

Some people will change, some will just stay where they're at. Everybody has a pain tolerance. Everybody has a level where it's time to change, because they can't handle this premium anymore. But again, we're not pushing them to change. We're providing the information.

Roger: That's great. This has been a fantastic interview. I could sum up this interview in just a few short words for clients: Pick up the phone and call All Medicare Solutions, because these guys know their stuff. Or e-mail them at partdagent@comcast.net. So, thank you very much, both Shelley and Brian.

Chapter 2
HUGH HIMMELREICH

Hugh "Flip" Himmelreich is Vice President of Travel Leaders and the owner of Century Travel Service in Spokane, WA. A 50-year travel industry veteran, Hugh believes strategic planning and the ability to recognize and seize opportunities are the keys to successful travel planning.

Hugh has served on several boards, including The Society of Government Travel Professionals, Discovery School, and Daybreak Youth Services.

Hugh is passionate about travel, fishing, and golf and specializes in planning hunting and fishing trips.

Roger: Hugh "Flip" Himmelreich is Vice President of Travel Leaders. This is a topic people should be excited to learn about. Why don't you tell me a little bit about how you got started in this business?

Hugh: My father was a pilot in the war as well as a commercial pilot with Continental Airlines. I started with Continental Airlines after he retired in 1967. I've been in the travel industry a little over 50 years. I was with the airlines for 16 years then I came into the travel agency side in 1984. I worked for five years for an agency in Boise, Idaho. Then, my wife and I bought this agency in February 1989. Next year will be 30 years we've owned this business.

Roger: Tremendous. Quite obviously, a lot has changed during that time. What would you say to people who are looking to travel during retirement? Why would they come to a travel agent versus planning it themselves?

Hugh: There are several reasons. For example, I just had a retired friend come to us. He wanted to be somewhere warm from December until the snow is melted. He has property that requires a lot of maintenance in the winter, such as plowing. If he had to book his travel himself online, it just takes forever. There's so much information to glean through and unfortunately, not all of it's true. That's the biggest challenge. Not just finding the information but getting the right information.

People that are retired have a lot of time to spend doing research, which helps us. It helps when they know a lot of specifics of what they are looking to do and what type of place they are looking to stay at. We can counsel them on what they want. Then we take that conversation and look at solutions based on their budget and figure out what price point they need to be looking at. Once we get to know a client, then when we see a special come through or something we think they may want to do based on our previous conversations, their bucket list if you will, then we can contact them to see if these specials are appealing to them.

They'll be on our mailing list and it becomes a relationship like other professional relationships, like your CPA, or your physician. We have a lot of people who depend on us to find the deals. And we have them. We get new deals almost every minute.

Roger: That's excellent. You've obviously traveled quite a bit around the world. What are some of your favorite destinations?

Hugh: I'm a warm weather guy, so I go to the beach. I have an affinity for Mexico. I speak some Spanish and I have lots of friends in different places. I used to spend a lot of time in Central America. I've been to Europe, Australia, New Zealand and all over the South Pacific, but I tend to like a place where the beach is white and the water's warm.

I love the history of Europe, but it's just really busy and expensive, and it takes too much time. I can get to Mexico or Hawaii and back in three or four days. Whereas Europe, you really have to have some time. It helps to be retired, and I'm not yet.

Roger: To paint a picture for the readers, we're conducting this interview on the coldest day so far this winter. It's that bone-chilling cold out there.

Hugh: It is. On our sign out front, we like to put up the name of some beach somewhere. This time of year we see a lot of people say, "Hey, it's time to get out of here for a week or even just a long weekend."

Roger: What are some of the current trends in travel that readers might be interested in knowing about?

Hugh: Let's take cruising. Over the last 20 years, the average per diem price for a seven-day cruise has gone down, on average, to around $100. That is very inexpensive when you think about the fact that you're getting food, transportation, entertainment, and a place to stay. Holy mackerel. How do you beat that? You can't.

But, the downside of that is they have started to charge for everything on board. Now you have automatic gratuities, so no matter what the level of service is, you pay the same amount of money for gratuities. They all have specialty restaurants. If you want to eat in any of them, it's a $20- $40 upcharge for the meal. Of course, there's a casino, and gift shops, and shore excursions, and alcoholic beverages or non-alcoholic beverages.

Except for your drinks with dinner, there's a charge for everything now. It didn't use to be that way. So what you find is people think they're paying $700 for the week and they're really going to pay $1,100 because all that stuff's extra. We have to counsel that. Unfortunately, people who are booking online are booking themselves, they don't really understand what all those charges can be. And that's unfortunate, because they get there and they're disappointed. As travel consultants, we make sure they know everything they need to know and what it's really going to cost and how they should budget for that.

The other side of that is the all-inclusive hotel or destination market, which is in the Caribbean and Mexico for the most part. They are literally all inclusive. Everything's included: alcohol and non-alcoholic beverages, all your food and non-motorized sports, etc. Once you buy your vacation, there are not a lot of other costs involved. We always make sure they know, "What's the real cost of your vacation?"

Roger: That's interesting with cruises. I wasn't aware of those changes. It's been a long time since I took a cruise.

Hugh: It's not every cruise line. There are some upscale products that are still "all inclusive". But for the most part, the mass marketing cruise lines, we're not going to use names but everybody knows them, that's the way it is.

Roger: How many travel consultants are there in your office?

Hugh: We have 14 travel consultants. Some of them service government contracts, managing travel for the federal government. We have corporate specialists who just serve businesses, and we have leisure specialists, or there's a combination.

Roger: As travel consultants, do you get perks? Do you go places and learn about various resorts, beaches, foods, and all that?

Hugh: Absolutely, but it's not all it's cracked up to be. In the industry, they're known as "familiarization" trips.

Hawaii, Australia, New Zealand, those kinds of destinations will offer familiarization trips. Hotels will offer either accommodations or meals.

Typically, when you go on one of these trips they're sponsored by the destination or an airline or maybe a hotel chain. An airline will reduce the fare to get you there. Then you go and visit a hotel property, and they'll buy you a meal, show you around their property and all the amenities. You familiarize yourself with their product so you can go home and sell it. That's kind of how it works. You might see three or four or five hotels a day. It's not like you're sitting on the beach with a cocktail. They're really working vacations.

It's the same thing with cruise lines. They'll offer reduced rates so you can go and experience the products, then come back and sell it. Very seldom is it free. It's normally at a reduced rate, around half price or sometimes a little less. But again, if it's a cruise, you have the same costs as every other passenger. That is never discounted. That's where they make their money.

Roger: Of course, you're familiar with those places after the trip. Can you think of a time when a familiarization trip helped you put together a perfect vacation for someone?

Hugh: Well, I can tell you that I have learned every time I go somewhere. I went to high school in Hawaii. I spent a year and a half there and have been back many times with groups, so I know the islands extremely well. The first time I was on Maui, there were two hotels in Kaanapali Beach. If you're familiar with that now, it's like Miami Beach. There are hundreds. It is helpful experiencing the "Aloha" spirit of the islands, being able to look at that whole island chain, being able to plan. I can ask somebody, "Do you want to spend a lot of time on the beach? Do you want to play golf? Do you want to spend time at some of the museums seeing the history and Pearl Harbor?" You have to go to different islands for different experiences. You wouldn't know that unless you had experience, or spoke to someone who did.

The other one that comes to mind was the first time I went to the Yucatan peninsula and went to Chichen Itza, which is one of the major ruins there. The only way I can compare going to that ruin is like going to the pyramids in Egypt. It's amazing, and I think the pre-Columbian history there would be pretty hard to explain or sell without actually experiencing it. I've sent lots of people there saying, "You can't miss this. Cancun is wonderful, lots of beach, lots of party, lots of things, but don't miss the history and the culture." To me, that was much more experiential than sitting on a beach with a cocktail.

Roger: That leads right into my next question. I love history and learning about cultures. I haven't traveled as much as I'd like to. I definitely want it to be a part of my retirement. Are there trips that people go on that include educational things or experiences they should take in? Is it included?

Hugh: When people come through our doors, that's what they're looking for. They don't just want to see locations, they want to experience everything those new places have to offer. When they go to Italy, they want to learn to cook Italian food. They don't want to just drink, they want help squish the grapes with their feet. That's the kind of experiential travel we're seeing. We're seeing lots of "I want to dive. I want to climb the mountain. I want to be on the zip line. I want to be part of the experience." Especially the food and wine thing for the retired people, it is a little less active adventure, but still immersion in that culture. Many cruise lines have those kinds of programs. We've put some together. We've partnered with a winery to sponsor those sorts of things, because that's the kind of travel people want.

Seeing is one thing, experiencing is another. The days of following the same old itinerary, day after day, are over. The "If it's Wednesday it must be Belgium" kind of thing. You're unpacking your bag every day and you don't know exactly where you are, it all looks the same after a while. Now we have a little more time spent in destinations actually seeing, touching, feeling, and being a part of things. Those experiences can be pretty high adventure. You have to kind of think about an African photo safari as being one of those things, like seeing and doing and staying in the camps, versus watching the National Geographic channel.

Roger: Do people make a point to come in here after trips and tell you about them? Do they send you pictures? Send you thank you cards and emails?

Hugh: All of that. And flowers. Well, not me but some of my employees. It helps when we're able to go and see and experience a destination, maybe more than once. We have people who are Australia specialists, African specialists, Europe specialists, Hawaii, Mexico, Caribbean, because they've gone and seen and done. When you can come back and provide someone with the information they need to plan their trip around what they want to do, and they go and enjoy that and have those kind of experiences, that's invaluable. For some people, a trip to Africa or Europe or wherever could be once in a lifetime.

It's awful to go somewhere and not have the hotel you need or the view you wanted, or the experience you desired, or to be able to do the kind of things you wanted to do. If you want to see the Vatican, you need to know when you can do that and how you need to do that. For example, my wife didn't get to see the Vatican because the Pope decided to do something else. As it turned out, she got to see the Pope, which was probably more important to her than actually seeing the Vatican, so it turned out great. But sometimes you can't do things you planned on, because there are certain functions or other things happening. It's all those little things, "the devil's in the details."

Our job is to know and understand the destination and understand the destination. I'm a great fan of Zihuantanejo, Mexico. If you want to go deep sea fishing, say you want to have a chance to catch a sailfish, I know the guy to send you to, because I've been fishing with him 50 times and I've never missed. I can tell you when the best fishing is. Knowledge like that exists in every one of these offices because they've been to these destinations and done what there is to do. That's why we specialize. Just like a physician will specialize in a certain area of medicine. They do a good job in that area. There's an old saying, "If we were all pitchers, there wouldn't be a ballgame."

Roger: That's good. If somebody reading this is retired or about to be, what would you say to that person if they had some inclination to travel, but didn't know how to get started? Where would be a place to dip your toes in the water? What would you say to motivate them to take that first trip?

Hugh: First, passports used to take two weeks. Now it takes longer, sometimes six weeks, depending on when you apply. So don't wait. Get your passport now. Because if you're retired and flexible with your time, then you can take advantage of those specials. If you can go off-season, you can go when the cruise line is looking to sell those last 20 or 30 cabins. Or when the airline's looking to sell those last seats, or the hotel's looking to fill those last rooms. That's when the specials are. It's all about supply and demand in the travel business, like it is everywhere else. That's why these online companies like Priceline exist, for distressed inventory. It's coming to a point now where occupancy is going up and up as the economy is better, and those discount places are struggling. They're struggling mightily, because the inventory is not there, and they can't offer that deal anymore.

There's other competition to that. Air B&B is a big competitor because of availability that's never been there before. And they can't market against it, because they don't know what it is. We don't know what it is half the time, trust me. That's part of the problem with that. You have to have a sense of adventure to go and stay there. You don't know the people whose house you're staying in. My daughter just went and spent three months in Hawaii doing an internship with the Pacific Whale Foundation studying marine biology. She stayed in a house belonging to a woman who would sit in her bedroom every night and bounce a ball against the wall for her dog. You never know.

Roger: Sweet dreams. The travel world has changed so much.

Hugh: But those opportunities are there, both good and bad, if you want to experience culture. Both my daughters spent some time in Europe and stayed in hostiles or Air B&B's. It was great, because they had locals helping them with food and culture and directions of what to see and do. It's a great way to do it, but you have to be willing to be very flexible.

Being flexible lets you take advantage of all those things. And for retirees who are looking to get away from the weather for longer periods, those things can be pretty good options compared to a hotel or a timeshare.

Roger: So if somebody came in to see you, and described some of the things they're interested in, do you keep that in a database and when those specials come along you contact them and let them know?

Hugh: That's right. We do it a couple ways. We have email blasts and magazines that go out every other month. When we get those specials, we either put them up on our sign, or we'll send out an email. Also, agents know where their clients are looking to go and will let them know when there is a special for those particular destinations. We have thousands of people on our mailing list. But each agent probably has 50 regular clients they've dealt with over the years.

It's a different world for retirees. It used to be, you might buy a little cabin on the lake or a timeshare in Hawaii, or a home in Arizona, and that's where you went for vacation. That's what you did every year.

Now, people want to see more than the same place every year. Some of the timeshare companies allow you to move around, so that's a little bit better. But what we're seeing now for retirees is early retirement for some lucky people, and more adventurous travel. They want to see and do and feel and touch. They want to experience things, rather than go to the same place every year.

Roger: We all know the traditional places to go: Hawaii, Mexico, Fiji. Are there some parts of the world that are trending? Opening up their arms to visitors?

Hugh: People have shied away from Mexico a little bit, because of political and drug situations, and I understand that. I've been there a lot. Trust me, the gangs are not after American tourists. We haven't got enough pesos for them to bother with. It's about rival gangs and the government.

Costa Rica and Belize are pretty hot right now, because they offer the same sort of thing. They've got the Mayan ruins, the beaches, the warm weather, they've got the same things Mexico has. They're a little more expensive. They're not as big, there are not as many destinations, and they're not quite as "touristy" if you will, but still probably hotter destinations than Mexico right now because of that.

Alaska's a big thing for us in the summertime. It's been really popular. I think with global warming, people want to see the glaciers before they're gone. I've been there quite a bit. The cruise market in Alaska is very hot these days, especially in this part of the country because you can drive to Seattle, get on a ship and cruise to Alaska. That interests some people.

Roger: Of your travels and personal experiences, do you have any strange travel stories you might want to share?

Hugh: I think we get a little jaded. There are probably things like losing your bag that would be a big deal to some people, but not to me. You know that's going to happen sooner or later. It's like Russian roulette: you check your bags six times, one time it's going to get lost. It's the average. So, you pack enough in your carry-on so you don't care. If you go where I go, where it's warm and wet, as long as you've got a swimming suit, you're good.

One time I went to Tahiti and they had me do the Tahitian dance. I was not drinking alcohol, but it didn't matter. I sprained my foot badly doing that dance, so I got to spend the rest of the vacation bandaged up, hobbling around the beach, which kind of ruined it.

But I've had to be careful. I guess it's about knowing your destination. There are certain resorts in the Caribbean, especially Jamaica, that cater to adults only. To a point where some of them may have areas that are clothing optional.

Roger: Surprise!

Hugh: If you don't know that, and you send somebody there, that could definitely be a problem. We actually had a guy come in and book through Hedonism. From the name you ought to know what to expect, but he booked the reservation there for him and his wife for a week, and away they went. When they arrived at the hotel, the wife immediately called the travel agent and raised all sorts of Cain about the fact that they were at this place where everybody was naked except for them.

Of course, we had given him a brochure. He knew. He didn't bother to share it with his wife. Hoping, of course, that she'd get in the mood or who knows what. But she did not, so we had to make other arrangements.

Roger: That's hilarious.

Hugh: It was kind of funny. That sort of thing happens, even accidentally. Although, I think that was on purpose.

Roger: That's a great story. Thanks for sharing. It almost sounds like the beginning of a novel. "Honey, ry. "Honey, now that we're on the airplane, I've got something to tell you…"

So I love snorkeling. Where would you send me for the best snorkeling on the planet?

Hugh: Most recently, I took our two daughters scuba diving in Roatan, Honduras, but you can snorkel there too. Those are some of the most beautiful corals I have experienced other than Tahiti. In Tahiti, you don't even have to dive to see it. The lagoons on the islands are sheltered, so you don't have to worry about the great big fish. You can literally paddle out and relax and just float with the current. Thhen paddle in, walk down the beach, paddle back out and float again with the current.

It's probably the most relaxed, beautiful thing because you don't have to worry about running into anything. It's shallow enough that you can see, but deep enough that you don't have to worry about running into coral. That was in Moorea and Bora Bora, where it was some of the best snorkeling I've experienced.

There are obviously places in Hawaii. If you get away from the beaten path, there are some great places to snorkel. I would have said some places in the Cancun, Cozumel area, but they got hit by the hurricanes not too long ago, and they're still coming back.

Other than that, obviously the Great Barrier Reef is some of the best in the world, but it's a long way away. I'm talking about somewhere you can get to in five hours. But if you can get to the northern part of Australia, the Great Barrier Reef would be a bucket list for a snorkeler.

Roger: You've planted some seeds for me. So you dive and snorkel. How long have you had Scuba certification?

Hugh: I'm not certified. I just go and do the resort thing. You can go anywhere and Scuba. It's called "resort diving." They put you in a swimming pool or shallow part of the ocean and run you through the safety check and tell you how to use the equipment. To me, it's like snorkeling but not having to come up for air. In my days before Scuba, when I only snorkeled, I would actually free dive down and take a look and go back up and rest for a minute and dive back down. That's what I like to do, and it's deep enough that there are things you don't get to see unless you do that.

With resort Scuba, it's shallow water. You're not going down hundreds of feet. You're going down 30, 40, 50 feet, maximum. It's less than $100 to go down for an hour in most places. I've done that in Jamaica, Honduras, Tahiti, Hawaii, Mexico, and other places.

Roger: It's very evident you have a passion for what you do. I would actually like to come see you and plan a trip, because I need to get out and see the world more.

Hugh: I would love to do that for you. There are a few things I would suggest, as you think about retiring and traveling. One of them being get an airline credit card. Take for example, Alaska Airlines. You can get a companion certificate every year for $99 to anywhere that Alaska flies. It is a great deal. Besides getting miles, you get that companion certificate every year. We have lots of clients that use those. You start creating those miles when you buy your groceries, tires, etc. Everything you do, you buy on that credit card. A lot of people don't want to necessarily run up debt, but if you pay it every month instead of writing a check, you create miles to use. If you do that, by the time you get ready to retire, you've got a few hundred thousand miles in your pocket. Then you can use those and get the most bang for your buck.

When you're in retirement, you can plan ahead and just go whenever you want. Sometimes the best mileage redemption is for tickets bought ahead of time, and sometimes those last-minute seats will be the best deal. So you can do a lot better in retirement using those miles than you would traveling during peak times, with everyone else. Those kinds of things can really make a difference if you plan ahead and do them.

Roger: That's a good tip. Is there anything we haven't touched on that you think would be a good addition?

Hugh: I'm 70 now, so most all my friends are retired but me. There are a lot of reasons for that, but I have traveled as much as I could since I turned 50. Because I didn't want to travel when I was 70 or 75 and have all of the restrictions. Whether it be health or medication or lack of ability to carry my own suitcase or just not having the physical ability to go and see and do the things I wanted to, like Scuba dive or climb a pyramid or a mountain or go on a zip line.

I don't recommend waiting that long to do some of that stuff. It's not all soft adventure and you need to be in good physical condition. Although, I think people are taking better care of themselves. We're living longer on average and doing more in retirement, but I chose not to wait. I've done a lot of things because I'm in the business, but also because I wanted to.

Roger: That's good advice, just get started. I hope you keep traveling and keep doing whatever it is you're doing.

Hugh: Absolutely. I take a group deep sea fishing to Mexico every year. I still escort groups when I can. I do love it.

Roger: It's a pleasure to get to know you and have you be a part of this book. I'm sure some people are going to pick up the phone and give you a call.

To contact Hugh:
http://spokanewa.vacation.travelleaders.com/
27 E Augusta Ave
Spokane, WA, 99207
(509) 327-9585

Chapter 3
TIM BRUMMETT

Tim Brummett is a certified personal trainer with Otis Fitness in Spokane Valley, WA, specializing in senior fitness and conditioning for weight loss. He is a graduate of the National Academy of Sports Medicine.

Like too many 50+ people, Tim slowed down and put on weight as retirement neared. When he retired, he weighed 360 pounds. But with the help of a personal trainer, he was able to lose an astounding 150 pounds in two years. That led him to get his certification and help other seniors who are overweight and unable to enjoy retirement.

Tim adores his wife, four children, and 12 grandchildren. He now has the health and vitality to enjoy every moment with his loved ones and wants to help you to do the same.

Roger: I'm excited to be here with Tim Brummett, who's a certified personal trainer. As we get older, our bodies change, and those changes can affect so many areas of life. Tim has a compelling personal story related to weight, health, aging, and lasting changes. Tim, please talk about your journey to become who you are today.

Tim: I'm 65 years old. I'm a husband and a father and a grandfather. Like many men, I became unhealthy and really overweight in my late 50s and early 60s. I just let it happen. I became diabetic, and had a really bad problem with my back. It started to affect everything. So at 62 I decided to retire, even though I had never intended to retire that young. The fire was still there, but not the ability to make it happen. I didn't know what I was going to do.

I weighed about 360 pounds. I knew I had to do something. The doctors all told me that, but I didn't have to be convinced. Anyone who has ever had to lose weight, knows it's easier said than done. It's an effort. Nonetheless, because my back was against the wall, I found a way that worked for me. I started to eat better, and I got active. I stayed with it, and over a two-year period of time I lost almost 150 pounds.

During that time, I was referred to a personal trainer. I was told, a personal trainer is not what you think. It's somebody who has been educated, understands your needs based on your age, and will create conditioning programs to help you lose weight faster and keep it off. My personal trainers had a big influence on me. I started to get into shape. All of a sudden, I could do simple things like go to the mailbox and back without being tired. So I thought, "I want to be a personal trainer. Why not?"

And so I went to school and got my certification, and today I'm a personal trainer. I have clients, and a business called Spokane Senior Fitness. My passion is to work with other people over 50 to make these kinds of changes in their life. It's much easier than a person thinks. If you have to lose 100 pounds and you're 60 years old, you think it's impossible. I say that's rubbish. Not unless there's something wrong. Of course, you can do it. My mantra is, "stay fierce," because that's what it takes.

Roger: How did you come about having such a positive outlook on fitness to communicate to people?

Tim: After going from being really overweight and out of shape to getting into shape, I can reflect upon it and say it is a journey. It's a journey I'm still on. It isn't something that happens overnight like the TV ads say. But unless there's some physical reason, unless you're restricted by a disability or an ailment or something that would inhibit you from putting challenges on your body to improve your condition, you can do what it takes. Even if you're in a wheelchair, you can start. I have to answer that question with my clients and with people I meet all the time. I want people to know, "It's not hopeless. Of course, you can do it, and here's why."

In the science behind conditioning, there's a principle called the "general adaptive principle". This is science. It's not a guess. It is the assurance to anyone that if they make the effort, they're going to improve. General adaptive principle means, if you put a stress on your body on a regular basis, your body will quickly and naturally adapt to that stress, and that stress will become the new norm, and you then have to put more stress upon it. One example is walking. You walk around the block and you darn near drop over, you're so tired. You do it a couple days later, and you're still tired. But the third time, it's not as hard. You keep doing it and it gets easier, and you walk further each time. Your body is quickly adapting. That's nature. When you put a stress on your body, you will adapt if you continue, which is the effort part of all this.

What's in your mind, your determination to get better, is the real test. But if you do it, you know you're going to improve. You're going to get better, and feel better, and you're going to get closer to your goals, if you stay with it, because it's a journey. You can tell I'm passionate about it. I had to do it myself, and I work with people every day who are worried they can't. But if they stay with it, they can do it.

Roger: Your picture is at the top of this chapter. People can see you're a very fit individual at 65 years old. But that didn't just happen from all the activities. You also mentioned the eating part of that. How do those two things work together?

Tim: Here's the reality of weight loss. That's about an 80/20 proposition. Only 20% conditioning, and 80% nutrition. That part is a lot harder for a person than going to the gym. They go hand-in-hand. One without the other is tougher, but if you do them both together, you're going to get there faster and with more motivation.

On my website, I have t-shirts that say, "Of course you can do it. Stay fierce." That's the mindset. "Stay fierce" is my way of life when it comes to my journey of losing all the weight. You have to learn how to eat. I say to people, "I'll prove it to you. Should you eat potato chips every night before you go to bed?" The same applies to cookies and candy and soda. The answer of course is, "No." Everyone already knows this. We live in a place that has conditioned us otherwise. We've grown up with it, it's in our brain. I've lived it. I understand completely. When you first start conditioning and losing weight, there is a point in the beginning where you have to develop a toughness. But if you hang with it for three or four weeks, that goes away. Things will happen in that first three or four weeks that will get you so fired up and so happy that you did this. It's just tenacity after that. Don't give up, because you'll master it. I really mean that. It's not a joke. There are no pills, there are no magic meals. Just eating right and activity, and you will get in shape again.

Roger: It's interesting, the culture we live in has so much access to unhealthy food sources. From fast food on every corner, to the grocery store. Sometimes I walk down the supermarket aisles and I'm appalled. It's just disgusting stuff. You have to go to the edges to find real food.

Tim: Let's face it, there are few things on the face of the earth that taste as good as McDonald's french fries. That's just the way it is. It's a bummer. There are some people that can eat and eat and eat and never get overweight. It's just genetics. It's the way it goes. But, most who overeat are going to have to pay a price with their weight and their conditioning. But we are conditioned in our thinking. Just think about it. Even today, our kids and grandkids are being conditioned by advertising. The food companies are just getting a little smarter, trying to sell more healthy food, and they're jumping on that bandwagon.

Roger: Tell me about a case of someone who has taken that first step. Someone who got in touch with you, and their lives have been changed.

Tim: I have a client who is 73 years old. I met her a little over six months ago, and we started working. We have worked two nights a week at the YMCA where I used to train. She had new knees, a new hip, used a cane and a walker, and had a desire to get better. She also was overweight. She had to lose that weight. I basically told her what I just told you. She said, "Okay," and she's been with me ever since.

I don't believe in stepping on the scales. The only true barometer when somebody starts this journey is to measure their body fat. The scale will discourage you. Remember the old adage, "muscle is heavier than fat." It's much more condensed. I would say she's lost six or more dress sizes. She no longer uses a cane. She can leg press 250 pounds. She can curl 40 pounds. She can overhead press 80 pounds. I'm very proud of her.

I will tell you, she's a warrior. She got that "stay fierce" part. Unfortunately, not everyone I work with does. The ones who do, because of general adaptive principle, of course they're going to improve. Even if they come one day a week, and they just quit eating junk. I usually start people off on the nutrition side with something very easy to do as a start.

Let's say you and I were talking, and your goal was to lose weight and get in shape. You can go on Google and find out the calorie count of what you eat on an average day. And don't cheat, have the correct total. Then start by removing 300 calories from that number. That can be as easy as drinking three soda pops a day instead of five. Just 300 calories. And come to the gym. Let's start there.

I know if I can just get someone for three to four weeks and they really do it, what's going to happen is, their clothes are going to start fitting more loosely. They're going to start feeling a little bit better than they have in a long time. Basically, that's all. Now I feel like my job here is done. You're going to stay with me and we're going to complete this together.

Now, if I have a client who has been with me for a month and has gained a bunch of weight, and they tell me they've done everything on the diet, I know they are fibbing, and I will call them out on it. I won't let that go the full 30 days. That's part of my job. I am always respectful. I love these people. I'm raised to be a nice person. But they have goals, and they came to me, and they are paying me for results. So while I'll try to do it nicely, I'm going to do what it takes.

Sometimes, I'll have to tell somebody not to give up. "You've put in two weeks. You can soar. You know what it's like, now. Don't give up on yourself after two lousy weeks. You're stronger than that. You need to expect more of yourself than that."

Roger: We can be our own best friends, and our own worst enemies.

Tim: We do try to make it fun. The real goal is to implement all these facts and all this knowledge, and then help them on the conditioning side, and help them get better faster.

Roger: Do you work with people individually, or in classes?

Tim: I work one-on-one sessions, I work two-on-one sessions, and I work in small groups, which are four people. Those are all personal training classes using each person's individual assessment. I design every workout program based on their goals, and what they can do. It's personal training. Obviously, one-on-one is more intense personal training, and where some people want to be. The other classes are really beneficial, and I usually tell people to start with a class. I don't want them to spend a lot of money until they really feel this is going to be right for them.

There are some people for whom exercise and conditioning just won't work. I don't want to have them spend money or get a membership.

Roger: So what would you say to a reader who's going over this section of the book right now, and has that stirring, and says, "Boy, he's talking to me." Maybe they've tried everything in the past, and none of it worked. What would you say to that person to get them to take the first step?

Tim: I would tell that person, "If you've tried other things that didn't work, you're probably more frustrated than you were in the very beginning." I personally have tried just about everything advertised. I ordered food that came to my door, and I tried classes, and I counted points, and I did all that. I couldn't live like that the rest of my life. That's the downfall of those things. They just are not realistic. Because all those diets are sensible low-calorie diets, and weight loss is calories in, and calories out. There is no magic. No magical combination of foods to accelerate your metabolism, no magic pills. I would tell that person, "You owe it to yourself to go to the gym and give it a chance." It doesn't have to be me. You can go to the gym where there's other people just like you. Every gym is going to give you a free session and assessment with a certified personal trainer. That would cost you nothing. The gym will give you a sample workout.

If they're a good trainer, and they're sincere, they're going to tell you this is only 20 or 25 percent of your journey if you want to lose weight. But it's an important part. I also don't want to discount the necessity for proper nutrition. And I want to let them know they don't have to torture themselves. Let's say you're on a 2,000 calorie a day diet, and you woke up this morning, and you ate a big bag of M&M's, and there goes your 2,000 calories. If you can go the rest of the day not eating, you will continue to lose. Stay with your conditioning, you'll lose weight. You just won't feel as good as if you ate something better. I'm sure you see my point.

Roger: What's the best life advice you've ever personally received?

Tim: I know exactly. It was from my mother. She said, "Don't *hope* to do well. *Expect* to do well." That's it. Do what it takes. That's the best advice I ever got.

Roger: It's good advice.

Tim: I think it is. My mother's still with me, and boy she was in charge. I tell people that all the time. If they just let my mom run things for 30 days, we would all be fixed up.

Roger: I like that. Personally, what do you like the most about the work that you do?

Tim: I like my own journey. I'm in the gym so I'm able to stay fit. I'm at a point now where I'm pursuing some pretty lofty goals for a guy my age, and that's really fun. Just the knowledge that I'm doing it after weighing 360 pounds not even four years ago, is amazing. It's just really fun.

I like being fit, and I like staying fit. I like all the new friends I've met at the gym, because they're just a nice crowd of people who care about themselves. That's the part I like the best.

Roger: What was your career prior to being a personal trainer?

Tim: I spent most of my life in the paint business. Selling paint, managing a paint store, and eventually I was district and then regional manager for a big paint company. Then I left that industry and worked with someone in the sign business for a few years. That was fun, and then I retired, and now I'm doing this.

Roger: That's an amazing story, and an amazing journey. You are definitely your own walking billboard.

Tim: Thank you. Another trainer teased me. He said, "You sure put together a heck of a long-term marketing plan. You went through a lot to get this advantage." I said, "What advantage?" He said, "You were really heavy, and now you're not. And you're old, and you did it. I can't ever do that." He's a young guy, and he's teasing me. I said, "Sure you can, in about 35 years. When you're 65." I teased him right back. I think I'm really fortunate. People ask me, "How did you really do it?" I say three things: I watched what I ate, I got busy, and God. That's how I did it. Somehow, someway I got fierce, and stayed fierce.

Roger: I would imagine all of us have to be inspired to get there. We don't immediately just change everything we've been doing without some type of an inflection point, a health situation, some advice, or a coach.

Tim: I wish there was a magic answer. There isn't. I wish I could look someone in the eye and give them some super pleasant way of saying, "This is the way we're going to do this." I can look someone in the eye, and say, "You're going to work. You're going to have an emotional roller coaster on the nutrition side. It's going to bug you. You're going to learn what 'stay fierce' is firsthand, and you're going to learn whether or not you can do it. If you're really are sincere, you will. If you're not yet sincere, I hope you'll remember me and call me when you are." That's what I tell a lot of people.

Roger: Would you say that sincerity of being ready to change would be the defining factor between somebody who finds success, and somebody who just goes through another cycle of trying, and failing?

Tim: I think it is. If you have to lose 20 to 30 pounds, that's not going to bug you enough. Someone who has to lose some weight because it's affecting their life is more likely to be motivated to make that change. It could be a 21-year-old youngster, whom I really feel bad for, because of their self-image. TV's full of sleek and slender models, and dudes all cut up and all macho. That's what we're raised with. It's not fair, but that's the way it goes. That's probably the biggest motivating force. That's the hardest part for myself: image. Most of the time I was probably wrong. I was too hard on myself, but when you're really overweight that's how you are. I was really hard on myself. I didn't talk about it. A person that has some weight to lose is going to have to encounter that.

The other type of client I get is the senior who doesn't necessarily have a ton of weight to lose, but they've really gotten out of shape. Usually they hit the wall. They were smokers, partiers, and drinkers. They have to get in shape. They have to learn what "stay fierce" is. They're happy, but now they're paying the price. They are 65, they have COPD or heart issues. Things have happened. Those are the ones that have a harder time understanding "stay fierce" than the person I work with who is wanting to lose weight and get in shape. A lot of those people had a fun, happy life. I get it, but they can't do that anymore, and they never worked out their whole life. That was their lifestyle. They didn't know what it was like to really sweat, and work.

An overweight person will come to the gym and work their heart out. I usually have to tell them, "Stop, slow down. Let me check your heart rate." This is a critical time.

I'm pretty passionate about all this because I just know anyone can do it. I see people walking down the street. I wish I could go up to them, and say, "Young lady, I know how you feel. Here's my picture from four years ago. You don't have to be like this. You don't have to do this. I'm not trying to get business with it. Go to the gym, get your free session with a personal trainer, and turn things around." I wish I could do that. I would be punched out, but that's how I feel about it.

Roger: So, you're changing lives one person at a time. How much are you enjoying it? You're healthy. You probably added another 25 years to your life.

Tim: It's the most fun thing I've ever done. A guy who saw me in a magazine for weight loss asked me, "What is your biggest motivating factor?" I have 12 grandchildren. The oldest is 20, the youngest is eleven. I want to be around to play with my great grandkids. I don't want to just be here. I want to be fit and active, and well enough to do fun grandpa stuff. That's my number one biggest motivation right now.

I'm going to compete in a Spartan race, in the 65-and-older bracket. I just want to get through it and survive. It's an obstacle course, and it's just ridiculous, but I just have to do that. That's another motivation right now.

Roger: That's great. Tim, this has been a real pleasure. Your content is powerful to say the least.

Tim: I'm kind of blessed. I just made a change. The people who contact me and want to work with me are out of shape. This traditional gym is really intimidating to them, even the YMCA. Some people do better in the smaller gyms with the smaller traffic, where there's not a bunch of unbelievably fit people running around. I was looking for the right gym, and I found it. It's a little remote, but my clients will find me.

For those who wish to work with me, it's called Otis Fitness in Otis Orchards. I know it's out of the way, but when I came across it, and I met them, they asked if I would I be interested in doing senior fitness there. I saw what they were doing, and I thought, "Man, this is where I want to bring my clients." The intimidation factor is a big thing for the first step. It's a big thing to get over. Maybe the biggest.

Roger: I could see that. I admire your philosophy, helping people to break through those first few weeks with the "stay fierce" model. After that, it seems it sort of takes over. "That's my new me."

Tim: It is, and I did it. Weight loss seemed really hard along the way. But when I look back, the first thing I think is, "Why didn't I just do this a long time ago? What was the matter with me?" Because it's not that hard. Every single person who reads this that wants to lose weight, or if they're over 50 and out of shape and they're worried, I would say to them, "The only reason you aren't where you should be is because you learned differently."

Roger: Tim, thank you so sharing your inspirational story, and such great advice. You'll have a positive impact on our readers.

Contact Tim Brummett at:

11427 E. 24th Ave.
Spokane Valley, Washington
Call (509) 879-7598
https://www.otisfit.com/training

Chapter 4
KORRIN FOTHERINGHAM

Korrin Fotheringham is a Registered Dietitian/Nutritionist and founder of Northwood Nutrition in Spokane, WA. Korrin works with children and adults with various medical diagnoses including eating disorders, digestive disorders such as IBD, diabetes, and food allergies and intolerances.

Korrin also works with primary care providers and utilizes nutritional counseling and motivational interviewing, and maintains a non-diet approach to nutrition.

Roger: Korrin Fotheringham is a nutritionist with Northwood Nutrition in Spokane. Just to set the stage, in financial planning I see people who could use nutritional guidance. For example, folks who get declined for things like life insurance, disability, and long-term care insurance, which require a client to be somewhat healthy. I also see people who struggle with overspending on food, particularly eating out at restaurants versus cooking at home.

Korrin, I want to ask you about the things you can do in a holistic way to help people with nutrition. But first, let's talk about you. What inspired you to become a nutritionist?

Korrin: I remember sitting at my kitchen table with some close friends. We were in our early twenties. I had just finished my undergrad. The world was my oyster, I could do anything I wanted. My friends and I were sharing a nice meal and I remember one of them saying, "You know, if I could do anything, I would go back to school and become a nutritionist or a dietician." We started talking about it, and so many of the things she was passionate about just rang true with me, and how I felt about food, and how I wanted to make a difference by working with people. Previously, I had worked in labs. I was very isolated, not talking to anybody. That's what I thought I wanted to do, but actually that wasn't the case at all. So, considering a different career where I could actually talk to people face-to-face, and feel like the words I was saying were actually impacting them in a positive way, that was really my source of inspiration – to feel like I was making a difference in that way.

So I went back to school after that conversation, and I took that dreaded biochemistry class that I didn't take as an undergrad because it was now a prerequisite. I went back to grad school, and I did it. That was the turning point.

Before then, I had really gotten into gardening. I had never really done any gardening as a child, but in my early twenties I had this great backyard with these raised beds, and I grew zucchini and tomatoes for the first time, and just fell in love with the process of seeing a plant grow to produce food that I was actually eating and feeding to my family. Then, in turn, taking that next step and talking with people about that food and how that food can be nourishing and helpful to their bodies. I think a lot of our society feels food represents something bad, or scary, or something to avoid, or something that's not good for us. I always try to shift the focus onto food that really helps us feel good and that is nourishing.

Roger: Great. Were both the undergrad and the post-grad at the same school?

Korrin: My undergraduate was at University of Washington, and graduate education at Bastyr University.

Roger: So you came over from Seattle to Spokane. Then how did you get started in your career as a nutritionist?

Korrin: I was at the end of my maternity leave from my last child, and was deciding when I wanted to go back to work, and what I wanted to do. I had serious conversations with my husband about starting a practice. It's something that I always thought of doing, but was hesitant about diving right in and taking that risk. But a couple of my colleagues were huge supporters and encouraged me to just go for it. I actually just started my practice earlier this year. What I've been doing so far this year is just getting it going.

Roger: What does your client base look like? Who are you trying to attract to help out?

Korrin: My client base is pretty diverse right now. It's mostly young adults all the way up to retired and elderly folks. I just had a conversation with an 80-year-old man. He's looking to come in to work on his high blood glucose numbers, for preventing diabetes. I help my older clients with things like diabetes prevention or management for type two diabetes. I help my younger and middle-aged client population with general wellness, so I have some weight loss clients. I have a non-diet approach to working with those clients. Also, clients have come in with IBS, or inflammatory bowel disease. Other clients come in with food allergies, and we work on how to manage those food allergies in their daily life. I also have a large portion of my client population with disordered eating, things like anorexia, bulimia, or binge eating disorder. That encompasses the range right now.

Roger: That's interesting. This book is probably going to be read by quite a few people who are nearing retirement, or in retirement. And regrets are a big thing: financial regrets, family regrets, and dietary regrets. I think we all have them.

If somebody is contemplating, "Why should I pick up the phone and call Korrin?" or, "Why should I pick up the phone and make an appointment with a dietitian?" what would you tell them, and what would you describe that path to look like for them, to help them out?

Korrin: That's a great question. It's so hard, because I feel a lot of people come from so many different backgrounds and histories. And just from working with people in relation to food for so long. Everybody has a history of food. It could have been the way they were raised, and their parents saying they needed to finish everything on their plate before leaving the table. It could be they were heavily into sports when they were a kid, and they needed to eat enough food so they could perform well in their activities. Or it could be their grandparents always gave them sweets, but they never got sweets at home.

All those kinds of things that happen as a child develop into something when we're older. It could look like a million different things, depending on the person. But I think that history we all have with food impacts our relationship with food later in life. I think there's a large variation for what "normal" looks like in our society for your relationship with food, and how you eat food, and enjoying food, and making food at home. But some people get outside that normal spectrum of food intake.

If you're thinking about calling me, I would think about: What are some things you're worried about with respect to your relationship with food? Are there things where you feel, "Gosh, I don't know if this is really normal. I don't know if this is detrimental to my health. I don't know how I feel about myself after I eat this certain something." There are just so many things to consider. That's why I love the work I do, because it's so complex and I really get to know the people I work with. There's just a lot that goes into it.

Taking those five minutes just to think about yourself and your relationship with food, how you grew up, where you came from, and how that's impacting where you are now with respect to how you are around food, and maybe some things that you struggle with in relation to food, can have such an impact. Those are all things I love to help people with, and talk to people about. I want to help them manage their food intake, so they can have a healthy and wonderful relationship with food the rest of their life. A lot of people feel food is just taking over control of their life, and they're just on autopilot around certain foods, and they just eat, and eat, and eat, and can't stop. It doesn't have to be that way. If you look at those things, and take a moment to consider those things, you can break the cycle and move forward. Maybe it could prevent a chronic disease later on. Maybe it could prevent developing diabetes. Maybe it could prevent high blood pressure. There are all those sorts of things that lead to long-term chronic diseases that can be really detrimental in terms of their health down the line.

Roger: That's great. When you talked about normal eating, it reminded me of one of your blog posts earlier this year. As a financial planner, sometimes I see people come in with financial statements that just make me cringe. I imagine when you walk into grocery stores and you see that 80% of the stuff is just packed with crap, I imagine there's that same cringe-worthy moment.

Obviously, you have a passion for what you're terming, "normal eating." Elaborate on that. What is that? What does that look like for the average person?

Korrin: My personal definition of normal eating is having flexibility with food. I think being flexible and having balance in your life is really important, and when it goes outside that normal spectrum, I feel there are regrets as you were talking about. What we more commonly talk about is feeling shameful or guilty for eating something, and leading to a cycle of other behaviors. Or it could be just like this rigidity, where people feel they have to stick within this particular line, either diet or some kind of lifestyle, where they aren't able to experience other things outside that particular diet. That rigidity is one of the warning signs I see when I work with people. And maybe it impacts their social experiences. They can't go out to eat with other people. Maybe it impacts, once again, how they feel about their food and their relationship with their food.

For them, it might just be a way to fuel their body. But I a normal relationship with food has so many aspects other than that. It's a wonderful thing to share with other people, it's a way to connect with individuals, it's a way to show love in your life with cooking with other people or cooking for other people. Food is so much more exciting than eating to nourish our bodies. I feel like that's my definition of a normal relationship with food.

Roger: You also enjoy presenting cooking classes. Tell me some of the feedback you've heard from people who have gone through those classes.

Korrin: I love doing that. It's one of my favorite things in my practice. I think a lot of the feedback I have heard from folks is just thinking about food in a different way, trying new foods they haven't seen before. One of my favorite things I love to do cooking demonstrations with is Napa cabbage. It's a Chinese cabbage that not a lot of people are familiar with. It has this really crisp, delicious texture and flavor. I like to introduce new foods. That's fun, to make it exciting, and bring something that people haven't always seen or experienced or tasted before.

The other feedback I've gotten is just how to integrate other foods you're not used to thinking about into a salad, for example. What are the different components of a salad that make it interesting? It's not just lettuce and dressing. We need some other things in there to satisfy all the aspects of our taste buds, and to satisfy the visual aspect of what that salad looks like, because you eat first with your eyes, not your mouth. What does it smell like? Using all the senses. My cooking demonstration really gets people excited about food, and that's my goal.

Roger: On your website, you describe yourself as a foodie. What's your favorite type of food?

Korrin: That's a really hard question for me to answer. I think I just have to say a blanket statement of Asian food, just because I love traditional Chinese food, I love Thai food, I love Japanese cuisine, all of that. All the flavors and different traditional foods in Asian cuisine are amazing. I haven't tasted something that I haven't liked.

Roger: Me, too. Can you think of the craziest thing that's ever been put in front of you?

Korrin: When I was younger one of my best friends' family was from Malaysia, so I have definitely had sea urchin before. And I enjoyed it. But I haven't had it recently, so I can't say whether I would like it now.

Roger: I mentioned earlier how I talk to people who are trying to manage their budgets with food. It seems to be the easiest thing to get out of control and back into control. I find that people take a guess at how much they spend. So what's your advice there? How do you work with people in terms of managing money for food?

Korrin: That's a great question. That's something I feel everybody, myself included, can improve upon. I think you're right in the fact that our culture emphasizes eating out and having these experiences around food because they're enjoyable. You can sit and enjoy the atmosphere and people's company and this great food, but it's also two, three, four times as expensive as that same exact meal at home. Unfortunately, the shift to eating out has been so extreme many people no longer have these wonderful spaces in our home to share a meal with people. But that doesn't mean that we can't do that anymore. I really encourage folks to just set aside a very strict budget for eating out. I think people are surprised at first at how quickly that goes away. If you eat out once or twice a week, depending on where you're going, you can easily blow through $100 very quickly in a week.

I definitely encourage people to eat more whole foods at home, because that is a much more reasonable way to live, especially on a fixed income. It can just be so challenging to go out to eat and include that in the budget. Just choosing things and going to farmer's markets is something I love to recommend, because you can share that with other people like you would a meal going out to eat. You share the experience of walking through a farmer's market and seeing everything the farmers have to offer. The wonderfully fresh fruits and vegetables that are grown nearby. That's a way to reduce cost because often times, things at farmer's markets are much more reasonably priced. They're coming straight from the farmer. There's not the middle man and you're supporting those farms directly.

So that's a way to reduce your costs. Also, shopping the sales and the whole foods aisle at the grocery store. I'm always recommending whole foods to folks I work with because they're the most nutritious foods we can have in our life. Whole food means it hasn't been processed. It's not been packaged. Things haven't been added to it or taken away from it. Check out your bulk foods aisle at the grocery store. The bulk greens. There are so many wonderful foods in those bulk bins. Yes, it takes a little longer to cook them, but with the Instant Pot sensation that's going on nowadays, it's not that much longer with pressure cookers. So that's a great way also to reduce your food budget. Just start experimenting and cooking food at home, and looking up new recipes and playing around.

Roger: That's good advice. I would say the majority of my clients are pre-and post-retirement. So, let's think about 50-years-old as maybe a line of demarcation here. As people get north of 50 as I am now, what are some of the things we have to make sure we're doing as we get older in terms of different nutrients? Maybe adding certain things to our diets or subtracting certain things?

Korrin: I wouldn't say anything really needs to be subtracted. But adding things is really the most important way to go about your food intake as you get older. Adding foods that are really nutritious. They give you the most bang for your buck in terms of nutrients, vitamins and minerals. Most Americans of all ages are generally low in fiber. We don't get enough fiber in our diet. And that can be really challenging for retired folks because their digestion suffers as a result. Increasing the amount of fiber doesn't mean you have to eat your weight in vegetables every day or eat vegetarian or vegan. It means you need a consistent intake of fruits and vegetables. It could be fresh fruits and vegetables or dried fruits or frozen vegetables when they're out of season. That's where a lot of our fiber comes from.

And as I mentioned before with the budget friendly foods, you could also do whole grains and beans. Those have plenty of fiber as well. Having them as part of your daily diet will make a big difference in fiber intake.

I would also make sure you're getting enough omega-3 fatty acids. I feel a lot of people have heard of these recently, but they don't necessarily know a ton of good food sources for them. Nuts are one of them, so walnuts are a good source of omega-3 fatty acids. Flax seeds, chia seeds are as well. Those are the teeny, teeny tiny seeds. You can find them in the bulk food aisle, but sometimes they're in the refrigerated section because they're high in those fatty acids, which are an oil, and when they're refrigerated they don't go rancid. Those are some good sources. Also, think of the wonderful fatty fish that's high in omega-3. Salmon is great. So are the small fish that not everyone can tolerate, sardines. Those are all really good food sources to incorporate, and ensure that you're getting those essential fatty acids that are great for cognitive function and your overall health.

The other main concern I think of is calcium. Calcium doesn't always have to come from dairy. I think in our culture we just always associate calcium and dairy, but there are other sources. Calcium is also found in really high amounts in dark leafy green vegetables. Kale, Swiss Chard, Spinach, and Bok Choy are great sources of calcium as well as broccoli. You can get it from dairy, but you can also get it from those dark leafy greens.

Roger: That's great. Korrin, you've shared a lot of good information, and there are probably dozens of other things we haven't even touched on. People who are in the Spokane and Coeur d'Alene area where you're working can reach out to you to learn more. What about people reading this book who live outside the area?

Korrin: I work with people virtually too, so there's always that option. Tele-medicine has come a long way.

Roger: All over the globe. That's tremendous. Thank you for the input you've given our readers.

Contact Korrin at: www.northwoodnutrition.com

Chapter 5
MEGAEN PALADIN-CHILDRESS

Megaen Paladin Childress is the owner of Paladin Childress Law Office, PLLC in Spokane, WA. She works with business owners and individuals, focusing on estate planning, elder law, Medicaid, probate, contracts, and small business formation.

Megaen provides education to the community through seminars on topics such as retirement housing and Medicaid, estate planning for non-traditional and blended families, and families with health issues.

She is a member of the Washington State Bar Association, the Spokane County Bar Association, the Washington Bar Association's Elder Law Section, Probate and Real Property Section, Business and Corporate Section, and the Spokane Estate Planning Council.

Roger: Megaen Paladin Childress is an estate planning attorney in Spokane. Estate planning is a very important part of any life plan, yet so many people seem to neglect it. Megaen, what holds people back and what should they know to motivate them to take action?

Megaen: I find that most people avoid or neglect to do something like this because of the topic at hand. You're talking about having to put yourself in a situation where you've passed away or you've become incapacitated. A lot of people don't want to acknowledge those things. They don't want to acknowledge their mortality or the fact that they could get sick. I've also had other people avoid it for superstitious or religious reasons. They feel if they essentially plan for death, that means they will die very soon. So it's often the children coming in and saying, "No, Mom or Dad, I need you to take care of this."

But in the past five years that trend has switched, and I think it's because we have the Baby Boomers. I'm usually dealing with people who have just administered Mom or Dad's estate, and they're in their 50s or 60s and are saying, "Gee, I don't want my children to go through what I just had to do, so I want to get this taken care of." So I feel the tide may be shifting a little.

Roger: Interesting. That's a similar conversation that a lot of Baby Boomers have with me around long-term care planning. I hear those same words: "I don't want to have anybody go through what I just went through."

Megaen: Many people are outliving their mind but not their body, and they're seeing the cost of care that comes with having to be placed in a facility to meet their care level needs. You're talking $12,000, $20,000 a month, and they say, "Eek!" So they call people like you and me. I think the conversation is getting a little easier.

Roger: What inspired you to become an estate planner?

Megaen: I was inspired to go to law school because of how adept I was at research, and then pairing that with my passion for helping others. So law was a natural choice. Then I honed in on estate planning partially on purpose and partially because that's what suited my talents. I always wanted to be a transactional attorney, but I wanted to work in intellectual property law back when I lived my big-city life in Seattle.

Then, I met and fell in love with my husband in law school, so we stayed here. To meet my transactional preference, estate planning and business transactions obviously were the best choices here. Then as it turns out, because I come from a big Catholic family, I've just had people pass away and I see what needs to happen. The way the women in my family were raised and react, we were the ones that would bring the casserole, make the phone calls, and hold people's hands. I've watched my mother and so many women in my family do that and it became a fit that I didn't know was obvious until I started practicing. I thought, "I really have the temperament for this." So I make it very easy for my clients to talk about something they don't want to talk about.

I also have that big family experience of knowing how different heirs will react, and the problems and issues that can come up with estate administration. Now that I'm practicing and doing probate litigation, I have extensive knowledge in how problems arise. I can use that for my transactional practice, and help with, "How can we avoid this? How can we make it better for everybody?"

Roger: How long have you been doing estate planning?

Megaen: Five years. Before that, I interned in appellate law and family law, and then I did a little bit of estate planning. That's what helped guide me into making this the focus of my practice.

Roger: And you have two toddlers at home, so I won't ask what you do in your free time.

Megaen: I don't have any. That's laughable, thank you, that's very funny. But no, I don't have free time.

Roger: One day, it will come along. I think about philosophical anchors when I think about really good businesses, like financial planning firms and estate planning firms. What are some of the philosophical anchors that set you apart from other estate planning attorneys?

Megaen: That's an excellent question. I think what sets me apart, and one of my guiding mantras for my practice, is access to legal information. I think it's unfair, just in general with all law, that people feel they can't pick up the phone and get the information that they need from an attorney because they're overwhelmed or they're intimidated, or they think it will cost too much money. I know that I'm highly trained. I know my education was expensive, but that doesn't mean that I should be a barrier between someone getting the information they need.

I like to be someone who freely gives whatever general information people need, and especially when it comes to something that's so necessary and practical such as estate planning. Just the practicality of, "Who's going to take care of me if I become incapacitated? Who makes decisions? Who's going to pay my bills? And then after I pass away, who's going to go through my things and make sure they're donated or given to the right person?"

Regardless of who you are or how much money you have, those are very practical questions that will have to be asked. It's important to me that people have that information. I like to tell my clients I "arm them with information". Then my job is to apply that information to their specific situation. Whether they hire me or not is up to them, but what's more important to me is that they're not intimidated by the process, or they don't feel lost. So that guides me in everything I do.

Roger: That's tremendous. It is a similar type of thing in my field. I've been in financial planning for 25 years and

I come across advisors and planners who say, "Oh, I won't work with somebody unless they've got X number of dollars." I just detest that. If somebody wants help, I'm there for them, to help them learn. Whether that's myself or someone else on my team or whoever, they're always welcome in.

Megaen: I hear that a lot. People say they don't need assistance or everything is simple because they say, "Oh, I don't have an estate." Maybe they think they don't have very much in terms of assets. First of all, I just don't like that way of thinking and it sounds like that's in line with you, Roger. Second, that doesn't make them any less sophisticated or any less worthy of receiving help than someone who, in their words, "has an estate." Especially because there's so much wrong information out there, in addition to the fact that there's just so much information out there. So, it's important for people to visit people like you and me. It's like a Reader's Digest. They can do a Google search or they can come and get trusted legal and financial advice so that they know they're in good hands.

Roger: And they get listened to.

Megaen: Yes, exactly. So they don't feel so alone. There's a ton of information out there and frankly, some of it's not so great. Sometimes it's hard to tell which is which. But that's why I went to law school -- so you don't have to guess or figure it all out.

Roger: Some people reading this book might be saying, "They're talking to me." What would you say to motivate them to take the first step, to maybe just pick up the phone and call you, or to send you a contact email? Maybe they haven't done anything about their estate planning. What would you tell them to motivate them?

Megaen: I would tell them to remember that they're hiring me. So they're the client. They're in control. Just as when you would hire a plumber or a babysitter or whoever you hire normally, most people remember they're the employer in that situation. So if they don't like something that's done or they have questions, they're okay asking or terminating the relationship. People feel the opposite power balance when they think of attorneys. It's not true.

To take the first step, it's okay to call me and feel me out, and to call other attorneys. It really is important that you hire somebody you feel comfortable with, and not just go with anyone because you assume it's all complex legal stuff that's way above your head. A lot of people get this intimidation and fear factor, so they don't ask questions, they just sort of go with it. Or, they avoid the situation altogether. It's okay to look around, it's okay to ask questions, it's okay to disagree. It's your life. I go home and deal with my own things. You're the one in control. My job is to make the complex stuff easier to comprehend.

Roger: What do you like most about your profession and what you do with people?

Megaen: I like that I assist people in solving some of the toughest issues they're dealing with, and that I am a hand to hold and offer guidance through a murky time in their lives. People are typically coming to me because they are planning administration, or what should happen if they're sick. And that's an emotional situation. A lot of the times they're coming to me because they've lost someone, or their husband has dementia, and we're having to do Medicaid planning, or something of that nature. When they're in these tough moments, they're already not thinking as clearly.

I like to give someone the assurance that the burden is no longer on them. I like to see their shoulders visibly lift as the weight's been lifted off, because they know they can just give me what I need, and then just go home and be the wife again, or be the son again, and not have all those extra questions swirling around them on what to do. I just slowly guide them, very easily through it, with empathy, so they can focus on being a human being again.

Roger: That's great. They get that pressure taken off their shoulders. They know that a professional is taking care of it. Then they can focus on the important things for their loved ones.

Megaen: Exactly. Like I said, that's how I grew up. That's what I would be doing regardless of whether I was practicing law, so it's just nice that I get to do it in my profession as well.

Roger: You came from a large family in the Spokane area. Then you decided to go over and become a Husky?

Megaen: Yes, I did. I didn't even apply to Washington State, although I grew up an avid Cougar fan. I know the WSU fight song better than I know the UW fight song.

Roger: Well, this being a Spokane-area book, that should go a long way toward currying local favor.

What are some of the most common mistakes you see? People bring their documents to you. Maybe they've tried to do it themselves, or they've gone to a place that just kind of cranks out the same stuff every time. You see mistakes in other estate planning. How do you go about addressing those?

Megaen: You've hit on one of the common things I see. Sort of those trust mills or estate planning mills. Those are pretty easy to recognize because you can tell the plan wasn't really tailored to the person. They have way more language and provisions in there than the plan warrants. Or, it doesn't touch on some of the more specific needs of the individual. For example, if they have a disabled child. And that's too bad, because most of the time they've paid a significant amount of money. Sometimes those plans will work out, but you can just tell the person didn't get the individual attention they would need.

The other issue that I see come up a lot is misconceptions on things like estate tax. People come to me often and say, "I know the government's going to take a percentage of my estate after I pass away," but that's just wrong. In Washington, the estate tax threshold is over $2 million, and then federally it's well over $5 million, so that's a very small percentage of people. Then of course, you double that if you're married.

Roger: Yes, we would all like to have that problem.

Megaen: Exactly. That's the first thing. The other misconception is probate. People constantly ask me to avoid probate. They've just been given all these horror stories, or they had a bad experience in the past, and it was terribly expensive. Everyone should know that in Washington State it's very easy to probate your estate and certainly not any harder than administering a trust. In fact, often it can be way more cost-effective than a trust anyway. If somebody's trying to sell you a trust in Washington State, that should give you pause. It may not mean you don't need one, it just should give you pause. The probate process, like I said, is very, very easy and can be very cost-efficient. Again, to be armed with that information is important, because people really can be taken for a ride unless they inform themselves.

Roger: So, probate itself, isn't it somewhat necessary to kind of put closure on an estate?

Megaen: No, not necessarily. There are probate alternatives. The only major reason you absolutely have to probate your estate in Washington is if you have real property. If you have a home, or a cabin, or something like that. But there are exceptions to even that rule. So, again, that's why people look to attorneys like me—so I can help navigate all the potential options a person has to find the best and most suitable one for their goals.

Roger: In your meetings with clients, I would imagine you often hear the phrase, "I never knew that could be done."

Megaen: Absolutely. There are a lot of assumptions on how difficult either probate, or estate administration can be. There are assumptions that you need some fancy trust or document in order for things to be legitimate. Really, a good, old fashioned Will is as good enough for people with $10 as it is for people with $10 million. So, don't discount some options, or yourself, just because of some preconceived notion.

Roger: In addition to passing on accounts and real estate and things like that to family members, people with generous hearts want to include charities. What kind of strategies do you talk to them about?

Megaen: I get that all the time. Depending on where they're at with that Washington estate tax threshold, we'll determine when and how to gift assets to charity. For the majority of people, including a provision in their will that includes either a specific percentage or monetary amount to their designated charity of choice is sufficient. I'm always very specific on the charity and I include their address. Because there's an example where a person simply left a gift to "The Humane Society" in their Will, but then there were two competing Humane Societies in town, so there was a fight. And that's no fun.

So I'm very specific in that regard and my whole intent, no matter the client, is to capture exactly what they want in the best way possible. But if I advise a client of what I think is best and they don't want it, then I don't do it. That's not my job. My job is to capture whatever it is that you want, in a way that's legally sufficient.

If you're over the estate tax threshold, then we talk about lifetime or creating some other tax plan to reduce or minimize the estate tax, if that is what the client wants. You can do all sorts of fun and fancy things, but ultimately my job is to listen to what you want and where you want your stuff to go, and then tell you how to do that.

Roger: That's great. How do clients find you?

Megaen: I have excellent referral sources, so I don't do a ton of advertising. I get a lot of referrals from other professionals and former clients in town, and then from time to time, I will do a speaking engagement to the general public. It's done through my passion for people being informed. But most of the time, it's just people calling me and asking me questions, and then they end up coming in and becoming a client.

Roger: How does that process work? Do you have an initial consultation with people, or do they fill out a form? What's your process, and how long does it take from start to finish?

Megaen: When someone calls me, most of the time I get their timeline. A lot of people call me right before a trip and say, "I'm leaving in two weeks. Can you do it?" Which a lot of the times I do. But, for all new clients, we have an initial meeting and go over the basic information I need to properly advise them. That's their family and intended heirs and assets.

Once I know their goals, I tell them what their options are, and what I think is best for them. Then, when they choose their option, I quote a flat fee. The fee is representative of exactly what I'm doing for them. So they can call me and meet with me and do as many things as they need to do within that flat fee without worrying about the clock running if they call and want to ask a question or change something. I try to be very clear and open about fees and costs, so my clients don't feel like they're at my mercy and don't have any say in the matter.

So it's a very easy process. And at the end of the meeting, if they don't feel comfortable with me or the fee or the plan, or they want to think about it, then they just say, "No," and that's okay, too. I've honestly never determined an exact policy on whether I charge for an initial consultation, because most of the time the client ends up hiring me and the consultation becomes part of the flat fee, or the person pays a consultation fee voluntarily because they appreciate my time and the information they received.

Roger: What's the timeframe usually from start to finish, just on average?

Megaen: It depends on the client. If they are responsive, it takes me roughly two to three weeks to get the initial drafts out once I've been officially hired. At that point, as soon as the client gets back to me, we finalize documents and they come in to sign. So I would say on average, maybe three months. And that's only because the client may have some conflict or something of that nature. I just did one this month that only took 13 days.

Roger: Wow, that was a very responsive person.

Megaen: Overall, it really is client-driven. I can be very quick. But I will always be honest, and I will tell my client if

	I have a particularly heavy caseload at that time that will slow down my drafting. So, I try to be as transparent as I can with time so my client knows what to expect and when to expect things.
Roger:	So, if people are going to take a trip, they should get in touch with you well in advance?
Megaen:	It's preferable that we don't do things under an expedited manner. Because every so often, I will charge an expedition fee, because you're taking me away from my other clients, and because most of the time people realize, "This really isn't as simple as I thought it was going to be, because I didn't know there were all these cool things that I could do." They never knew about things like charitable giving or creating a special needs trust for their disabled grandson, or Medicaid planning. There are things we may or may not touch on in our initial meeting, and then they end up leaving with what I call a "Band-Aid Will," because they realized "Oh, I want to explore these options a little bit more," and we end up taking more time and finish things up when they're back.

So yes, I like to have a little more time than a two or even three-week turnaround, because I'm a wealth of information and people seem to enjoy that, and really like to explore things with me and that can take time. |
| Roger: | I'm picturing somebody reading this and seeing terms like "special needs trust" and "Medicaid planning". |

Talk to me a little bit about what those are and who needs them?

Megaen: A special needs trust is a type of trust that will protect the beneficiary from being kicked off certain government benefits if they came into money through an inheritance or settlement, for example. If someone is receiving SSI or Medicaid benefits, for example, and they were to receive an inheritance, they risk being kicked off the benefits because those are resource-tested benefits, which means you're only allowed to have a certain nominal amount of assets to your name. So a direct inheritance can be destructive to some people.

Let's say you have a child who is disabled and needs a high level of care, such that their medical bills without Medicaid could be in excess of $40,000 a month. If you leave money outright to them in your will, then they'll get kicked off that benefit and now they're spending all their inheritance until they're back down below the resource threshold and forced to reapply. And there may be a penalty period. So, what the special needs trust does is allows your beneficiary to have the benefit of their inheritance and keep their government benefits. Federal law allows that money to be protected from being counted as a resource against that beneficiary.

It's a great tool. Congress has created it for that very reason, so people can have benefits and a little stream of income to cover what the benefits do not, such as clothing and haircuts, entertainment, etc. This allows them to have a comfortable lifestyle without having to worry they're going to be kicked off their benefits. I love special needs trusts. and especially with the Baby Boomers and people needing that advanced level of care for situations such as dementia. With these trusts, you don't have to worry that if the healthy spouse passes away first the ill spouse will be kicked off their Medicaid benefits or forced to spend all the assets on care so he or she qualifies for Medicaid.

Roger: I so concur with that. Readers, if there's anybody in your family that actually has special needs who is presently receiving government benefits, or there is that possibility in the future, absolutely get in touch with Megaen or your own estate planning attorney, because it's very important.

Is there anything we didn't talk about that you'd like to share or include?

Megaen: I think the takeaway is that it's important to me and people like you to just let us help you, because we know how beneficial it is and how much time and agony we can save. There are cool tricks I have up my sleeves like special needs trusts. I can help with things that people stay up at night worrying about, not knowing there is an answer out there for them. So it's important to reach out to professionals in the community for help, and it is okay to create that team, to have your attorney, to have your financial planner and CPA, and make them work for you.

I think that's a good thing, and it helps everybody in the end.

Roger: Very well stated. Thank you for being a part of this book. I'm sure people are going to get quite a bit out of this interview. If you're reading this and you need your estate plan done, I would encourage you to get in touch with Megaen.

Contact Megaen Paladin Childress at:
Marycliff Financial Center
819 W. 7th Avenue
Spokane, WA 99204

(p) 509.624.4107
(f) 509.327.1181
https://www.pclawoffice.com/

Chapter 6
JULIE ADAMS

Julie Adams is the General Manager of Heritage Funeral Home and Crematory in Spokane, WA. Heritage Funeral Home and Crematory is a multi-award-winning company that serves all faiths, and provides a warm and inviting atmosphere for families to make final arrangements and hold memorable services.

Julie is a graduate of Chapman University and was Valedictorian of the Mortuary Education program at Mount Hood Community College.

Roger: Julie Adams is from Heritage Funeral Home and Fairmount Memorial Association. Talk about what that means.

Julie: Fairmount Memorial Association is a non-profit cemetery organization. The organization owns and operates seven cemeteries in the greater Spokane area. And they are the sole shareholders of Heritage Funeral Home, which is a for-profit funeral home.

Roger: Okay. So this book is primarily to help people plan for retirement, but it's also about how and where to seek advice, and what areas of advice people should look into. As I was putting this book together, I thought it should include somebody who's associated with end of life planning and funeral planning, because no matter what we do in our retirement, that's one commonality we're going to have to face.

Why don't we start with you telling me a little bit about what you do and how you got involved in this as a career?

Julie: I've been in the business for just over 12 years. When I started, I didn't know this would be my career path. I was a psychology major in school, and after graduation I was looking for something that would fulfill my desire to help people without owning my own private practice. My parents got some information in the mail about pre-planning, and as I read through the letter they received, I thought, "Well, this is the kind of thing I'm interested in, helping people without having to analyze their problems," so to speak. So my mother encouraged me to reach out to that particular funeral home and just talk a little bit about what they do. In doing that, I realized I was less inclined to do the sales and pre-planning side of things, but I was interested in funeral directing. Helping people when the need arises, or in an "at-need situation," which is what we call that.

I started off as an administrator and then moved into an office manager position over in the Seattle area. I worked there for about two and a half years and decided to go to mortuary school. I did that in Portland, Oregon, and that took me about a year, because I already had my bachelor's degree. After mortuary school I became a licensed funeral director and embalmer and worked doing that for quite a few years before I moved to Heritage, where I am now the general manager. So I oversee the services, embalming, meetings with families, as well as the day to day business operations.

Roger: Excellent. It's a beautiful facility too. I'm holding in my hands, your pre-planning and bereavement guide. Anybody in the Spokane area could pick one of these up. It's a great resource.

Julie: For that guide, we worked with advertisers who are directly related to the business, similar to this book, of course, to try to put something together that was not only going to be helpful when pre-planning, but also if a death were to happen. Questions like, "Who would I call for moving expenses if I need to move mom out of her home that she's been in for 50-plus years?" It has information about grief. And of course, there's a big section about pre-planning. "What does a burial cost? What does burial look like versus a cremation? What are my options for cremation?" We are trying to educate so you can make a good decision rather than just choosing based on cost.

Roger: And we'll get into some of those differences, too, but here's a question I have. What do you see? Because I'm sure you see both sides of this coin. You see people who have taken the time to really plan end of life events, and then you see people who have it just thrust upon them all of a sudden, without any planning. What are the differences in that? What's family A versus family B look like in those situations?

Julie: Well, I would first say let's add family C, which is the unexpected younger death, where someone just hasn't thought of those things yet, and they may have planned to do it 10 years from now. Those are unique situations. But if you look at someone who's around retirement age, and they have not yet planned, whether that's pre-pay or just putting information down for us, there's a lot more that goes into the process with that family.

It may be even easier just to say that when someone has come in to make those pre-arrangements, especially if they have pre-paid, that's kind of the cherry on top. But if they have at least come in to make the arrangements, for example, "I choose cremation versus burial. This is where I want my cremated remains to be placed," or "this is where I'd like to be buried," or those things, there's a sense of relief with the family when they don't have to think back on that conversation they had 15 years ago and know whether or not that's really what they wanted.

Because, in the cases where someone hasn't put those wishes down, that's what the family is left with. "Did you have a talk with mom? Did she want to be cremated? Did she want to be buried?" "Well, everyone in her family was buried at such and such cemetery, but I thought she mentioned cremation once." So there are a lot of questions, and there's a lot of room for not necessarily regret, but not knowing if you've made the right decision. It leaves people thinking, "Did I do right by Mom?" Or Dad, or their husband or wife.

If a person takes the time to come in and at least lay out a pathway for where their family should go, even just the very basic decision of cremation versus burial, it at least sets the path for success, in terms of having the family walk out of here feeling they've done right by the person who's passed.

Roger: Talk a little about the changes in terms of the directions of cremation and traditional burial

Julie: Well, we definitely see, here in the Pacific Northwest, that cremation is growing exponentially every year. We're at about an 80% cremation rate in the Pacific Northwest. Some countries are at nearly 100% cremation, just based on their traditions and things like that. But I would say societally, people think cremation is the least expensive, the least involved. I hear a lot from people, "Eh, just cremate me." First and foremost, it really isn't as easy as that. There's actually more paperwork involved with cremation. Typically speaking, it is a little bit less expensive, just because you have to put caskets somewhere and an urn requires a smaller place. But it does open up other opportunities for scattering or placement in your home or things like that, so you don't have to have a cemetery involved.

But we encourage people to always consider a cemetery option as a place to go and visit, especially with society as it is right now. There are so many commercials on genealogy and finding ancestors. I think back on the people who said, "We'll just take Mom home." She's probably still in a closet somewhere, or maybe she was scattered on property that they haven't marked. So 20, 40, 50 years from now, someone looking for their ancestors is saying, "Well, we know she died, but they didn't do anything to memorialize her so we could go back and check on where she was, or where she was laid to rest."

Roger: That's interesting. I bet a lot of people haven't thought of that. What you're saying is whether it's a traditional burial or cremation, you offer services that people can be here, at the cemeteries.

Julie: Yes, and for those families who are adamant about scattering in multiple places and not having part of the cremated remains at the cemetery, we still encourage and have the option of placing a memorial plaque. In other words, the cremated remains do not have to be here at the cemetery, but you still have a place for someone to come and visit and say, "This is where we come together to remember that person." That's a less expensive option and it just gives that spot for people to reflect and remember.

Roger: Yes, someplace to go and contemplate memories, and think. Regardless if somebody has a traditional burial or cremation, most still have the ceremony, the celebration of life, bringing everybody together for that memorial service, right? Is that a big part of what you do?

Julie: It is. For many, many years with traditional burials funeral homes were very involved in that process. Just for the sheer sake of having a person in a casket. We're the caretakers of that person until they're laid to rest. Cremation has opened the doors for people to go to different venues, to do celebration of life, or more of a party, or at a home. We still try to remind people that we are skilled at organizing events. That's what we've done for so many years. That's what we went to school for, to take that off of your plate. If you're going to have a service somewhere else, let us organize it for you.

We are event planners. That really is what we do. People don't think of a funeral as an event in the way they do a wedding. But we're moving chairs and organizing food and drinks, and the person who's speaking, and doing the microphone, and putting videos together, and ordering flowers. All those things that you see at just about any other event. Whether that's done here at the funeral home or a family chooses to do it somewhere else, we still are very interested in being involved, because that's what we do. We want to make sure people take the time to memorialize and to celebrate.

There's nothing more heartbreaking for a funeral director than to have a family say, "We're just going to take so-and-so home." They aren't planning to do anything. My personal opinion is every life deserves something, whether it's just a gathering of family members or a large celebration with 500 people. It depends on the person of course, but everyone deserves something.

Roger: That's good. Well said. Tell us about the various ways you use your facility.

Julie: We are considered a full-service funeral home. We've been here since 1995, so we're actually a relatively new facility. As far as what makes a full-service funeral home, we have our services here, we have viewing and visitation here. This is where we meet with families, of course. But this is also where our crematories are located, and this is where we do all our preparation work, which means embalming and things like that for viewing and visitation.

Roger: Everything is right here?

Julie: Everything is done here. I can say that although that's the goal of most funeral homes, there are some organizations that don't do everything onsite, so that's just a good question to ask. People should do their research with funeral homes. I always encourage them to just ask those basic questions. Because that type of thing may or may not bother someone, but if it does bother you to think that your loved one is going to be taken offsite to be cremated, then it's good that you know that, so you can make the decision not to use that facility. If it doesn't bother you, that's fine. It's personal preference.

Roger: How big is the actual cemetery here?

Julie: Here at Riverside Memorial Park, we have hundreds of developed acres and hundreds of unused acres.

Roger: So, you're not running out of room anytime soon?

Julie: No, we're not. As a matter of fact, because of the seven cemeteries and the locations of those cemeteries, there are some spots where we're actually considering selling off some of the land. Because as you look at the increase in cremation, you just don't need as much land for cremated remains. So we look at the increase in cremation, and the amount of land we have, and how long we've been here. We do the math to figure out, "Well, what does forever look like for us?" There's still a ton of land left over.

Roger: To give people a visual fix of where you're at, you're on Government Way, on the Bloomsday course. So no burials on the first Sunday of May? There would be 50,000 people coming by.

Julie: That's true. We can't even come to work that day. In fact, when a death occurs on that day, our hope is that they've passed in a place that will allow us to keep them there for the duration of the day. Usually our goal when someone passes is to go pick them up as quickly as possible and bring them into our care. But on Bloomsday, if someone has died at a hospital, we say, "Well, it's going to be a little bit before we're able to get to you, because we just can't get into work." The course blocks our gates.

Roger: I don't really know how to ask this question. You're seeing people at a very vulnerable time in their life, when they're going through shock, loss, grieving. What's the good side in that? What's the positive humanity that you see associated with that?

Julie: When people hear what I do, if they haven't been through the process themselves, they'll often say, "Oh, that's such a sad job." But often, by the time the family gets to the funeral home, it's well past the time their loved one died. Maybe they've had a night's sleep. They've cried, they've grieved, they've notified people.

I'm not a hospice worker. Those people are saints. They're there at the time that the death has occurred.

When the family comes here, they know they're coming here to do something good for that person, whether that's planning a service or putting an obituary together. By the time they get here, we're able to talk candidly about the person. A lot of times families are even willing to joke about certain things that may have happened. Sometimes if someone's been on hospice care for a while, they'll joke about, "Oh, gosh, every time so-and-so walked in, Dad did this."

They didn't feel comfortable doing that when he was still living. But now they're in this different mental state. When we get to talk about the services, we're doing a lot of reminiscing. It's a lot of, "Well, what kind of music did he like? What kind of activities was he involved in?" If we're putting a slideshow together, we send people home and tell them to bring back photos. Then I find that when people bring me back the pile of photos, they say, "Oh, gosh, that took way longer than I expected because we got to talking." You're looking through pictures that people probably haven't looked through in a long time.

It's a time when family pulls together and does that really great reminiscing. When they write the obituary together, or if they ask me to write the obituary and I'm privy to their stories, their banter back and forth about, "Should we put this in, or should we put that in?" It can actually be happy. It's such a good time for the family just to pull together and be thinking so positively about the person.

And that's really beautiful. There's always grief, and there are those pictures that pop up that remind you of something, it hits that little spot, somebody might shed a tear. Or they're sharing a story that brings them to tears. But, it's usually met with something beautiful, everyone gathering together and saying, "Yeah, you're right. He did this, or she did that. Okay, let's do this." That feeling of, "He or she wouldn't want us to be sitting here crying. Let's talk about this funny hat that he's wearing in this picture," or whatever it might be.

So we don't see as much grief here as I think people believe. There's a time for that, and I think when they come in to make the arrangements and are planning things, the service is one of those times where you take a step back and go, "This is their time. They're surrounded by people that love and support them." We're more of shadow people at that point.

Roger: You do a lot of important work. I've never really thought about some of these things. I imagine you would describe your career as very rewarding.

Julie: It is. It's extremely rewarding, because you're able to guide people through a difficult time. Most people plan maybe one or two funerals in their life. Usually one parent, because when the first parent passes, the other one plans it. So people plan for the second parent, and then usually a spouse.

So people don't have a lot of experience with this. But we do it every day. We hear the questions people ask, and we see the things that may or may not go wrong. For example, a lot of families think you need to do a service basically the next day. It's so urgent to them. "Well, we need to do the service as soon as possible." I usually encourage them to take a breath and think about it, because there's a lot that goes into a service. One of those things is an obituary, which will be in the paper, and of course online as well. So we help them with that.

But it's part of history. I have had families who've come in the day their mother died. They've already written the obituary and they want it in the paper for tomorrow. That's fine. But when it comes out the next day, they realize they forgot to put in an aunt, they forgot to put in the information about when Mom and Dad got married, and that Mom was very actively involved in this group or that cause, because they wanted to get it in ASAP. So I say, "Just take a breath. The hard part's behind you. But you're still in it. You have to come out of that fog to be able to see clearly. Let's make sure we have all the right people listed in the obituary. Let's make sure we've put everything in we to be that you want to be part of history forever." Sometimes you need to take a couple days to just let it sink in, and then go from there.

Roger: Julie, this has been so informative. I've learned a lot today. Is there anything you thought we should cover that I didn't bring up?

Julie: Well, I touched on this a little bit. I always encourage people to do pre-planning. But I should point out a couple things. One is that people often have a misconception that the funeral home and cemetery are the same. They aren't. Your cemetery plans are going to include your burial property. That's what we call the opening and closing, so it's the labor and mechanics involved in actually opening and then closing the grave. Most cemeteries require some sort of what they call an "outer burial container." That's like a casket for the casket. It's usually made of some sort of concrete or steel, and that helps maintain the integrity of the cemetery ground.

Older cemeteries have grounds that are sunken in. Our goal is to keep them as flat as possible. It makes it easier for us to maintain the grounds. Your headstone, things like that. So that's what your cemetery covers. That can be for casket or urn burial. There are tons of options for cremation. You can have an urn placed in the ground, and there are scattering gardens. So the cemetery covers all that.

But your funeral home is different. When a person passes, the funeral home will come out, 24 hours a day, 365 days a year. We'll pick up the person from where they've passed, bring them into our care, and hold them here until we have the necessary permits to either cremate or bury. The funeral home is the one that helps you with the obituary, planning that funeral or memorial service, ordering military honors for service and things like that.

Unfortunately, what sometimes happens is someone will be proactive, and when the death occurs, the children say, "She made her arrangements, we're good to go." But she didn't make the cemetery arrangements. And it happens the other way quite a bit, too. "She has her burial plan. Everything's taken care of at the cemetery." That's great, but there are no funeral plans. And the funeral home has charges as well. Because cemeteries are usually non-profit organizations, as ours are, and funeral homes are considered for-profit, we can't share an account. It's separate.

Roger: That's interesting. I had no idea.

Julie: A lot of people don't realize that. Fortunately, as a combination, we're able to walk our families through the difference. "Here's what this is, and here's what that it, and this is why you need both." So we try to get people the complete package. Sometimes people aren't prepared to make those arrangements and pay for those arrangements on the same day, and that's fine.

The other thing I'd like to mention is when it comes to pre-paying, we always encourage pre-payment for the cemetery, because that's property. If you want a certain spot, you need to pay for it ahead of time, or else you may not get the specific spot you want. That is very highly encouraged. On the funeral home side of things, although I do encourage pre-payment because there are a ton of fantastic benefits, we usually will guarantee our services price. So today you pay what our prices are today, and if you die 50 years from now, you're not paying above and beyond those prices. But more importantly, just getting something down about what you want. The funeral home will hold those wishes for you for no charge. We have what we call "information only" files. Those are for the people who may have made their cemetery arrangements, and they're not quite ready for their funeral arrangements, but they wanted things known. "I want cremation. I like the song *In the Garden*. I'd like these people to speak if they're alive and able and capable and willing. I'd like so-and-so to officiate." All those types of details can be put down and stored here for no charge, because even if they're not paid for, at least there's that peace of mind for the family that they're doing right by their loved one.

And then if you get to a point where you're ready to pay, we have different payment plans for that, too. It isn't necessarily a "pay all at once" thing.

But let me repeat, the big thing is that they are two separate things. In the cemetery we highly encourage to pre-pay, so you get what you want as far as location. The funeral home has a little bit more flexibility. There are benefits to pre-paying, but the biggest benefit really is just to make sure you have what you want down somewhere, so your family knows that in case something were to unexpectedly happen.

Roger: Absolutely. It's interesting, too, you talk about pre-paying for this, in financial planning it's a source of pride for our clients to say they've taken care of that. You can be talking about a million-dollar IRA, but that's not as important as, "I took care of my funeral arrangements and they're paid for." It's just a point of pride.

Julie: I see that with people a lot as well. "Oh, I've already taken care of mine." That's great. If I could, I'd give everybody a gold star for it. Because when it comes down to it, as we already discussed, it just gives your family this sense of clarity.

Roger: Well, the focus of this book is advice and you've given a lot of it, so thank you. It's been a pleasure talk to you.

To contact Julie:
http://www.heritagefunerals.com/
508 North Government Way
Spokane, Washington 99224
Phone: (509) 838-8900
Toll-Free: 1-800-475-0136
Fax: (509) 838-8942

Chapter 7
GREG & HANNA STEWART-LONGHURST

Greg and Hanna Stewart-Longhurst are the principals at Stewart-Longhurst Certified Public Accounting in Spokane, WA. Greg founded the firm in 1992, and Hanna joined him in 2013.

Stewart-Longhurst is a full-service firm that serves its clients business, tax, and financial needs. They offer unique business consulting and tax planning services on an ongoing basis, and believe building relationships with their clients is the key to a successful business.

Greg is originally from Idaho, and graduated with honors from Idaho State University with a BBA in Accounting. Hanna is a Washington State native who received a BS in Accounting from Brigham Young University. Together they have nine children and 10 grandchildren.

Roger: I've known Greg Stewart-Longhurst and Hanna Stewart-Longhurst for quite a few years, and we do a lot of mutual work together with clients. It's a pleasure talking to you both. Let's start by going back in time a little bit. Tell me about your personal roads. What inspired you, or what led you to become CPAs?

Greg: I grew up on a farm, and I wanted to be a farmer. I wanted to take over my dad's farm, to be his exit plan. I went to a trade school. I was in a farm crops management program, where I was learning how to weld, how to kill weeds, and mechanical stuff. One of the classes I took was farm bookkeeping, and I loved it. I got straight A's in it. I was working two to three weeks ahead of the class in the book because I loved it so much. It just spoke to me. My professor told me I should really investigate becoming a CPA. I took a couple years to think about that, and then I got serious about school. I saw it wasn't viable to farm with my dad from a financial standpoint and didn't want to starve to death. So I went to school, pursued a CPA, and I really love it. I'm having a good career with that.

Hanna: I came at it from a different direction. We both have a farming background, but I grew up knowing farming wasn't viable. My parents had eight children. They sent all eight of them to college and all eight left the farm. I started in college with a chemical engineering major, because I loved chemistry, but after a couple years I looked around and realized it wasn't a good fit for me for various reasons. So I started taking classes that sounded interesting. One was basic accounting. Interestingly, I found that most people really struggled with that class, but to me it made perfect sense right from the start. Although it was like learning a new language, it seemed like something I had always known and understood. I just had never seen it presented before. But it just fit. I loved it. I took another accounting class and loved it as well, so I just kept taking accounting classes and realized that was the direction I wanted to go.

Roger: Growing up on a farm taught you about hard work.

Greg: I was one of five children. Three of us were boys so there were a lot of farmhands, but my dad put the girls to work too. Gender didn't matter.

Hanna: Laborers were also in high demand on our farm. Even though farmers are kind of conservative and a lot of farm girls don't do as much farm work as the boys, it wasn't that way at my house. I was put to work.

Roger: The hardest days I've ever put in, in terms of actual labor, were helping on farms. I remember when I was 10 years old, in North Dakota, we were bailing hay and it was the hottest day I ever experienced. I thought I was going to die. Anyway, good job getting off the farm and getting into an air-conditioned office.

Hanna: That is the truth. Growing up, every other kid loved summer vacation, but we loved going back to school because it was a whole lot easier than the farm work over the summer.

Roger: You both took different routes to get to this firm. What were those paths like and how did this firm come about?

Greg: Right out of college, I took a job with Coopers and Lybrand—now known as Price Waterhouse Cooper, one of the largest CPA firms in the world. Coopers Lybrand was the third largest CPA firm in the world at the time, and they had an office here in Spokane. I was employed by them for two and a half years. It really opened my eyes. I was on the audit staff. We audited everything: from a mine company up in Wallace, to grocery stores, to high tech companies, to a Ford dealership. We got to see how large companies operate, how they keep their books, the standard of accounting, and tax work that they expect. After two and a half years there, I left and went to work in a paper mill north of Spokane. I was the finance administrator. I helped design their accounting system. It was a brand-new system.

Then I started doing taxes on the side, probably because I got bored. That really flourished and took off to the point where I couldn't do both my full-time job and taxes at the same time, so I put my shingle out and just grew from there. Hanna and I merged in 2013 and we've just kept growing.

Hanna: My practice came about while I was still in college. I determined that I just really loved doing tax work and that's what I wanted to do. After college, I worked for several years for other CPAs doing tax work. I loved it, but as my family grew, I could see that my children needed more attention, so I took a few years away and raised my children. When the youngest started school,

I put out a shingle and started doing some tax work on the side, like Greg. You kind of build it up on the side until it becomes big enough that it can take over. I started my practice on my dining room table and worked out of my home for quite a few years. The work steadily became more, and I steadily got busier. The work came in by referrals and such, until I was working full time. Then, as Greg said, in 2013 we merged our firms and came together to work.

Roger: You do understand that the phrase, "I love doing taxes," is pretty rare?

Hanna: I certainly do.

Roger: What do you like most about being a CPA and working with people?

Hanna: When people come to see us, they tend to be nervous, stressed out, and concerned. There are a lot of negative feelings around taxes. I'm able to help take away all their negative energy. I can get their information, package it up, and just take care of it for them. I can help them save money and help them get their tax return prepared right. They leave my office feeling confident that I'm going to handle it. They just leave so happy. They can go out and be incredibly productive because they've left all that negative stuff here. I just love that. I love being able to help people.

As much as people generally don't think of CPAs as really helping people, that's what I love about it. It's exciting!

Roger: Somebody reading this part may be worrying a little more about a situation than it warrants. And everything's always worse until you face it. So you would encourage people to just face their fears and take that first step, make a phone call or come see you, and bring their worst-case scenario.

Hanna: It's funny you say that, because a lot of times people are afraid to tell me what the situation is. They whisper it. They're really concerned. They have these fears and these concerns and it's so awesome that we can set those to rest.

Roger: That's great. Greg, what about you, what do you love the most about this?

Greg: The thing that came to me was from a couple of nights ago. We had this huge junk drawer in the dresser in our bedroom. Everyone has one of those. The other night, I pulled it out and dumped it on the bed. Stuff went flying everywhere. I put the drawer back completely empty and I organized all that stuff. If I didn't know what it was, or hadn't used it in years, or didn't want it anymore, I threw it away. Then I put the organized stuff back in that drawer. I really enjoyed doing that. That's just like a tax return. People bring in this huge box of unorganized stuff. They're not sure what's relevant and what's not. We have the ability to go through that box, organize it, and come out with a nice clean product that the IRS wants, and the client likes. We enjoy doing that. It's just a matter of organizing things.

Hanna: Yes, that's what it is. I just thought of a great story of a woman who came in to see me who was really in a lot of distress. She was older. Most of her friends and peers are probably retired, but she and her husband are still working hard. They've struggled financially and hadn't filed tax returns in a while. It was this big secret. "I've done this horrible thing and I don't know what to do about it." I can say, "Look, here's a plan. Here's how we can fix this." I can reassure her. Other times I have people come in and say, "I'm just so worried. I'm so afraid that I'm doing something wrong. Can you do my tax return for me?" Then they're just so happy we can.

I also had a man come in who said, "We just really need somebody who knows what they're doing to handle this. We know that we don't know." Every time I've spoken with him since, he's just as happy as can be because he's passed it off and he knows it's being handled.

Roger: As a financial planner, I always ask people what attorney did their will, or who their tax professional is. When they say they've done it themselves, I cringe. So let's get into that a little bit. In today's world, there seems to be a push towards do-it-yourself-ism in those areas. I certainly face that in the realm of investing, and I know you face it in the arena of tax preparation. Can you talk a little more about the good, the bad, and the ugly of that? It sounds like you're seeing people that might have gone down that road for a few years and then are afraid of what's happened.

Greg: Looking at the last few months, the real estate market has been growing and people are selling their rental homes. Invariably, almost every new client that did their own tax returns has messed up how they treated their rental home on their tax return. They didn't take the depreciation, or they didn't take the rental home at all, and they've lost a lot of deductions. We got several people a refund in the five-digit range, because they just didn't understand the tax laws or how to prepare a tax return. Turbo Tax is a good program, but let's face it, it's only as good as the person using it.

Generally, to correct someone's errors, especially with the IRS involved, costs more than to have done it right in the first place. That's kind of what we try to teach people. If you want to try to do it, that's fine, but if you get in trouble, then you're going to have to deal with the IRS and it's going to cost a lot more to fix it. Do-it-yourself doesn't always work. I used to change the oil in my car until the time I didn't do it right and all the oil ran out and it was everywhere. I'll pay somebody 30 bucks to do it now and I'll read a magazine while they do so. It's fine. There's a point in time when it just

	becomes smarter to have someone help you with things.
Roger:	I think the overarching theme of this entire book is helping people to discover the resources that are available for all areas of life. Whether it's a fitness coach, or health, or travel, or getting your estate documents in place. Certainly, taxes are a big deal because it's one of those things we all must deal with. The people that feel overwhelmed by it don't have the phrase in mind, "I love doing taxes." It's good to come to people that are competent in it and can also put an arm around somebody and say, "It's going to be okay. Let's get a plan put together here!"
Hanna:	We see it almost daily during tax season. People will say, "I was afraid it would cost too much to hire you to do taxes, so I hired somebody who was a lot cheaper. It saved me $300." Then we go through their tax return, and find that they missed $1,500 in tax deductions, and you think, "You saved $300, but what did it cost you?"

If you try to do it yourself instead of hiring an expert, it usually ends up costing more. I've found it wise to hire experts for things in my life that have technical elements to them. |
| Roger: | Plus, dealing with the IRS is something I don't think anybody should try to take on themselves. It certainly helps to have a professional when you do get that |

dreaded letter from the IRS or an audit or something like that. What type of skillset do you have that helps them through that scenario?

Greg: Over the years, time and time again I've seen the IRS have no mercy on people who are not represented by a tax attorney or CPA. People who prepare their own tax returns can go in and defend themselves in an audit and the auditor will rip them apart. Then they come to us because they've been assessed $10,000 or $20,000 or more. At that point it's difficult to go back and have the auditor change their mind. There have been audits where I've gone in and done nothing but sit in the room while the client shows their documents to the auditor and nothing has come up. Just the fact that they're being represented makes the IRS nicer, calmer, and more professional, it appears.

We specialize in representing non-filers: people who haven't filed in a long time. We're also affiliated with a tax attorney who helps us. We get their taxes caught up and take advantage of the various allowances the IRS has for people who are six to 10 years behind. Then when they owe a lot of money, and it's an over-their-head amount of money, the tax attorney can take over and help them. They have several different options there.

One of the greatest examples of that was a client who was a prominent local figure. He was real sheepish, just like a dog with his tail between his legs. He said he hadn't filed his taxes in three years and he was scared it was going to become public and be on the front page of the paper. He and his wife had a business on the side. I told him to gather all his receipts together and bring them in. They had a big garbage bag full of receipts. But it was in their car, and the night before their appointment, their car got broken into. The receipts were gone. They were devastated. They came in almost in tears, thinking this could be a career-ending move. But there are ways to work through that. There are things we know as professionals that people who are not professionals don't. We were able to work with the IRS in recreating his tax return and helped him get caught up and paid. He was much better at his job after that. That's why it's important to have professionals help you. That's what we're good at doing!

Roger: So, those people are obviously out there in our community. In the Greater Spokane area, there's well over a half a million people. How do you reach people? What do you do for marketing and who's the ideal client you're seeking?

Greg: The main thing that draws our clients in is my endorsement as the local provider for The Dave Ramsey Show. Dave Ramsey is a famous syndicated talk radio show host that deals with finances. As an ELP, Endorsed Local Provider, I have the exclusive right to his listeners in Eastern Washington. I'm the only person he refers to. I've been doing that for over

10 years. I know his people well, their nuances well, and what their expectations are.

Our ideal client is someone who's trying to get out of debt, is financially responsible, and perhaps is growing or investing in a rental home. They might have some mutual funds they're trying to sell or do something with. Or they're starting a little business. So usually a family or small business is a perfect client for us. Someone who's financially responsible, who also comes from Dave Ramsey is great.

Roger: With all the farming communities and your background, do you work with farmers as well?

Greg: We do. We have several. We have a farm out in the valley, and one down in Palouse producing a huge operation. I love working on those accounts. We have a lot of small farms too. We have people with 20 acres and a couple of horses who call themselves a farmer, and we help them too. Of course, we understand that stuff well, having lived it.

Roger: One of my farmer clients brings me a bag of onions every year. I'm thinking, "I don't know what I'm going to do with all these onions."

Greg: We had a cattle rancher who paid me in steak one year. He was appreciative of the service. It was dang good steak too.

Hanna: That's just how farmers work. That was always part of the deal growing up in the farm community. I grew up in an area where there were a variety of crops and people were always leaving a bag of carrots, or onions, or potatoes, or beans, or corn on somebody else's doorstep. Or just inviting their neighbors to pick all of whatever they needed for their family before harvest.

Roger: So, what are some of the modern-day challenges in running an accounting firm?

Greg: There are a couple. Number one is security. ID theft. Every year there are more and more regulations. This year we could not do a tax return for someone unless they had a driver's license. That was really irritating to many of our clients, but it's something the IRS has imposed on us. We have new passwords that must be changed every so often, even our own local software. We go to great lengths to secure the data of our clients, because we have their social security numbers, their names, and birth dates. We must take good care of that information.

The second one is just a shortage of good CPAs to hire. If you're looking for good help, it's hard to find right now. We need more accounting students that are qualified and want to do taxes. I think those are the two biggest challenges.

Hanna: Other things include the changing tax law. That's a continuous thing. We love that. We love studying it and staying up on it. That's not really a challenge for us, it's kind of the fun part!

Roger: It seems like every couple of years or even more frequently something changes in the federal and state tax laws.

Hanna: Over the years, there are things that have stayed the same about our industry and there are things that change. We know we're going to get new tax legislation, things are going to change dramatically, and everybody's going to be scared and worried. That's all part of the way it works. You see the pattern year after year. It's fun to be able to reassure people and help them understand how the tax law is going to impact them.

Roger: As long as I've been in financial services, there has been talk of simplifying tax law, but I've never seen it go backwards. It always seems to get more and more complicated. Professionals like you are always going to be needed. You're saying there's a career opportunity for people?

Greg: Absolutely. CPAs are in demand. Some of the bigger firms are paying signing bonuses. You would think it's like the NFL. If you're qualified, these are good times.

Roger: Excellent. I've learned some things today. And it's a pleasure working with both of you. If you are reading this and you're in the Spokane area, and you'd like to get a second opinion on your taxes, or maybe you're one of those people that has an issue and you're worried, Greg and Hanna are very safe. They'll give you honest, straightforward advice.

Hanna: Thanks Roger!

For more information, visit http://s-lcpa.com/
Or call their office (Call & Text): (509) 468-9617

Chapter 8
KEN BOHENEK

Ken Bohenek is a business broker in the Coeur d'Alene, Idaho area for Murphy Business and Financial Corporation.

As a former business owner, Ken came to Murphy with a desire to assist other business professionals. Through his experience with the transfer of businesses within his family and friends, he knows the importance of having a qualified broker involved. Ken comes from a family of entrepreneurs in businesses ranging from bars, restaurants and a plumbing & heating company established for over 38 years.

Roger: Ken Bohenek is with Murphy Financial. Ken, let's start with a little bit of background. Tell me about where you grew up, and what your childhood was like, and what brought you into this type of business.

Ken: That could be a whole other story. My family and I are originally from New York, but we moved out West. We grew up in Missoula, Montana. There are quite a few entrepreneurs in my family, and I essentially grew up in a family business.

When my uncle moved out west, he purchased a defunct plumbing and heating business in Missoula. He brought in my dad, and built it up to become the second largest shop in town, about 18 employees. Back in the '70s, my uncle was grossing over $1 million a year in revenue, which back then was pretty substantial.

Then my uncle went into the bar and restaurant business. My dad took over. He ran it differently, in the sense that he saw the struggles my uncle had with employees. He typically only had one or two. He ended up doing the vast majority of the things himself.

I purchased the business in 2003 with a 10-year plan. I wanted to be out and onto another venture. I met with a broker in 2006, and the experience was rather unsavory. The guy didn't do his job pre-qualifying before an initial meeting. It's pretty important, if you're attracting one of your competitors, that you make certain the competitor is qualified properly before you sit down and expose who the other company is in town.

Going forward, I said, "If I'm going to sell this, I'm just going to sell it myself," which I did. That was 2012. All my friends are self-employed. My brother's self-employed. My mom and her husband have owned a number of businesses.

So I sold my business and took a little bit of a break, but was actively looking at other business opportunities. I was actually looking at some businesses back East and also an opportunity in Arizona.

One day at a barbecue, I was introduced to a woman who was a Murphy broker. We got into a conversation about what I did, what I'm doing, and where I'm going. I mentioned that I had always loved the Coeur d'Alene area, and had friends there and in Spokane. She said, "You need to talk to Kevin Knepper," so she put us in touch.

What was interesting is around that same period of time, I received recruitment emails from two other brokerage firms back East, who said, "You're a buyer. Have you ever considered this industry as a profession?" I thought, "Maybe I'll take a little deeper look into this," and I met with Kevin. Then, after really doing some due diligence on the companies I was looking at, Murphy was by far, top of the heap. So I went with them.

Roger: I've heard really good things about Murphy. What is it that sets them apart as a company?

Ken: I know everyone says, "We have high ethics and standards." But Murphy actually does. They have a tremendous back support system, and industry experience that's unmatched. That was part of it. But I just couldn't find that anybody had anything bad to say.

We have a high closing ratio. I think part of that has to do with extensive training, and again, support. We have our own community. Nobody is going to know everything about every industry. But with us, you can put a question up in a forum, and somebody else can come in and say, "Here's what you need to do." Or, "Make sure you're doing this." Or, "Go to our library, and there's actually a research report on this particular company." There's advice on what to do when you meet with this prospective client, and so on.

Everybody works very well together. The fundamental foundation that the company CEO put into place a long time ago was "co-broke or go broke." Everybody in our firm works really well together. We have some really great people, and the great people make a great organization.

Roger: In order to help people understand what your world is like and what a business broker does, can you describe a recent success story, without using names, of course. Just the concept you walked somebody through and how that went?

Ken: The number one thing about this kind of business is setting expectations. That's a big one. And obviously, with that goes objections. You try to get as many of those objections, and expectations, and difficult questions done on the front end, because it really helps throughout the process. In this business, you never stop learning.

Here's a recent example. I had listed a service station. It was in a challenging location. The man who owned it with his wife, had just reached the end of his tenure. He wanted to retire. The station had actually been in their family for about 80 years. None of the kids wanted to take over. I wish I could have met with them a few years prior. He was doing okay in terms of the things he should be doing, but not everything. For example, he owned this real estate. But he wasn't paying himself a rent.

I had the listing for about a year. There were challenges. But in the end, we got a good buyer, and we were able to qualify him. It was tenuous at times, but we got the deal done. Ultimately, we got the business sold.

My client was able to fulfill his goal, which was to retire. Now they're traveling. They're car nuts like I am, so they do a lot of car shows and activities. They have friends they travel with.

Now he has time to tinker in the shop when he wants, and they can enjoy their grandchildren, and just enjoy life. It's really pleasing to me to be able to help somebody get into the next chapter of their life, and put some money in their pocket in the process. Now they can enjoy it.

Roger: I'm thinking of my clients who own businesses. Obviously they include the business in their retirement planning, but oftentimes they've done little to nothing in terms of preparing that business for a sale.

Even if we're talking about assets and liabilities, and I ask them what they think their business is worth, it's hard for them to come up with that. They don't know how to put a value on that.

Ideally, when is it good for someone like you to be brought into that situation? How do you coach people to go from building their baby, to starting to think of it in terms of an exit strategy that's going to help them retire? Because it can be bigger than their 401(k) or home equity, and be a very big part of their retirement.

Ken: The sooner the better, really. Take estate planning. People will begin estate planning long before they figure there are any health issues or anything like that. You can be doing your business in conjunction with that. You can literally structure the deal to flow right into your will, if you chose to. But it's really never too early.

Those who plan well typically will have us come in and do a valuation. Sometimes it's just a matter of benchmark information. Here is where we are right now, today. Here's where we're trying to get to. It gives them a path to get there.

We do offer consultation services. The other great thing about doing this, especially if you have a goal in mind of maybe selling two to five years down the road, going through a lot of the processes of getting a valuation done will set you up for a similar circumstance with all the due diligence that's required from a buyer and seller when you have a business under contract. It gets a business owner accustomed to, again, expectations. They know what to expect in those environments, so they aren't saying, "Why do they need to see this? We don't understand that."

Sometimes the owner isn't quite in the financial place they want to be, and we can explain to them why you should be paying yourself a salary, how it benefits you. Payroll taxes added back in and how that computes out, what it looks like to a buyer. If you own the real estate, why you should be paying yourself a reasonable rent and how that factors into the lending process, especially with SBA.

SBA is going to impute a reasonable owner salary, period. People don't understand when they take draws, how it affects the value of the company, versus if they're paying themselves a salary, and it's hitting the P&L. It's really important to do that early. Even if they're not ready to sell for quite a while, they know there's some housekeeping on the financials that's going to need to be done, as they go forward and are deciding to sell.

Roger: You were talking about your experience, where you had one of the plumbing and heating businesses in Missoula, and then the word got out that it was for sale. In a small town, that can be devastating. So talk a little about the importance of your role, and the confidentiality around that as well.

Ken: Well, fortunately at that particular time, in '06, word didn't get out. In 2011 when I was working with this other buyer, we tried to keep it hush-hush. When I bought the business, for whatever reason, it was just intuitive, nobody got my cell number. There was a woman in the office who basically filtered out the calls, and if there was somebody I needed to call, she would contact me. Because my thought process was, I knew I wanted to sell in about 10 years. As involved as I was, the ability for me to be in the background and doing all the things that needed to be done with employees and whatnot, made more sense. Because I just envisioned, "Well, if I want to sell this, I don't want to be so ingrained in the business that I am the business." I didn't understand what closely-held businesses meant at the time. I just knew that if I'm a factor pulling the strings, and tomorrow somebody else steps in, it's seamless. Well, that's what I ended up doing.

There were customers of mine that contacted me even a year later, and said, "I had no idea that you had sold." We're really big on confidentiality. We take it very, very seriously with everything. So it's the first thing we do with prequalification of buyers. But if you have a listing that's out there for a while, or somebody does say something, you get it. I remember one night, I was out to dinner, and a guy I had known for years, who was a friend of my dad and my uncle, was sitting at another table. I stopped to visit for a moment. He said, "I heard an odd rumor that your company's for sale." I said, "Jeff, if you handed me a duffel bag full of cash today, you can have it."

I think it's important to remember that if it comes up, just roll with it and deflate it. Because what else are you going to do? Even as strong as our confidential agreements are and what we do, it's really hard for me to turn around and try to pin a breach of confidence on someone else. But oftentimes our deals close, and people don't know that the business is sold.

Roger: How do you coach a business owner who is basically the face of the business? Their clients look at them as the person they're doing business with. If they're going to sell that business now, the clients don't necessarily have trust in the person's that coming in. How do you suggest they begin to make that transition?

Ken: There's one I sold last year that was like that. There was a lot of personal good will. The company was started by the seller, from scratch. He built it up to be extremely profitable in a short amount of time. Every situation's different, but in that case we just extended the amount of time the buyer and seller were going to work together. Because this industry is relationship-driven. The buyer and seller need to get along throughout the process because every deal will dictate different terms. In this one, we had a 30-day agreement in place with a possible extension period beyond that. Part of that was, after closing, the buyer and seller were basically going to be going out and either calling on accounts, or making introductions to repeat customers.

It was a construction-related business, which is a volatile industry anyhow. I wanted to make sure the buyer had the most success possible. Especially since the buyer moved himself and his family from across the country, and didn't know anybody.

Every deal is a little bit different. In the case of the service station I was talking about, the buyer had a tremendous amount of previous experience. The buyer and seller actually knew one another. The relationship aspect of it wasn't really a problem. The buyer had a lot of experience, so he was able to just jump right in like it was nothing. But in that other deal, there was a tremendous amount of goodwill in that company. That's where the buyer gets nervous. "How do I know that when the seller leaves, people aren't just going to leave with him or find somebody else because they don't know me well?" I will respond, "Then you guys might need to work together for a while."

Typically, that's one of the other important aspects of seller notes, because the seller has the best of interest in that business and its ongoing success. Sellers typically perceive the seller note as problematic or, "I don't want to do that," or they look at all the "what ifs". But buyers look at it like, "The seller has a stake in the game, so he's got the best interest in my success." And that helps mitigate some of the risk for the buyer, so it's very important.

And you might have a situation. I'm working on another deal that we haven't engaged in just yet. It's quite large. The seller already knows he may need to stick around six months on a transitional period. It all depends on the complexities of the business, the size of it, and how much goodwill really is in there with the seller. Again, relationships are important. You might need to work with the buyer for a considerable amount of time after, to ensure his success, especially in those kinds of businesses.

Roger: What are the things you like the most about what you do in your career?

Ken: I like the negotiating aspect of it. I love hearing the stories of people and their businesses, because I've always been interested in business. Whether it's somebody that purchased a business from somebody they didn't know, or from a family member, or they started it from scratch, everybody has a different story. That's really interesting to me to hear about.

I do enjoy business-to-business dealings the most. I've got a really strong customer service background. I love doing business to consumer. But I've always liked business to business a little more because it seems like we're on that same field. We've all had the experiences, both the joys and the not so happy moments of small business ownership. But everybody's got a story and it's always interesting to hear.

Roger: How do you acquire clients? Or how do clients find you?

Ken: Actually our company as a whole is working on some rebranding and remarketing. Because it's amazing, I believe we're the second most successful brokerage firm in the country right now, and most people haven't heard of us. So we're on a mission to correct that. Most people find me through referrals, and web presence. We do networking, different mailing campaigns, and whatnot. There isn't any one path to meeting clients. It's a business that, like yours, requires quite a bit of trust. So that's why referrals are really good, from networking and previous clients, and being able to garner that trust.

Roger: That's good. When I travel, people in business circles will ask about the economy out here and what makes it go. The interesting thing is, Spokane, Coeur d'Alene, probably even over into Kalispell and other parts of Western Montana, it's not like we have a giant Boeing plant or Amazon or Microsoft that's sustaining the economy. I think here, the hospital's probably the biggest thing. But how would you describe the economy as you meet with these various, kind of hidden-away entrepreneurs? How would you define the tapestry of our economy out here in this part of the state?

Ken: I'm still surprised when I get a call or speak to somebody who is working with a client on a company you didn't even know is in your backyard. There are a lot of those. There are a lot of companies in Spokane, Coeur d'Alene, even up into Sandpoint, in those areas, that have relocated from other areas or just started, that you don't even know about. For the longest time I didn't even know Lighthouse Dressing was in Sandpoint. I saw them for years in the supermarket, and then when I moved over from Missoula I said, "Wow, they're in Sandpoint."

But there are a lot of companies that do things around here. I think in Spokane, especially the Coeur d'Alene area, there's a quality of life aspect. I know of a large performance company that started in California and ended up moving their operations up to Coeur d'Alene. And that was really their thing. The owner wanted to provide a better life for his family. So they moved the business up here.

Roger: You came from New York. Was that move based on quality of life?

Ken: That was part of it. And some of it was the economy. The economy was doing really well here. It was in a slump back there. So it was both. I can tell you, my mother was not happy about it. And my parents still crack about certain things in Missoula, food being number one.

I still remember, we had just moved here. The movers hadn't brought our stuff yet. We were in our new house, and we were hungry, and my parents decided to get a pizza. You probably see where this is going. My mom threw a cloth over a box, and we sat down and we each grabbed a slice, and my dad said, "They call this pizza?" Now, when I go back to New York, I always say, "Now, this is pizza!"

But it was good. There were things my family missed about there, but there were a lot of benefits to growing up where we did.

Roger: So let's say a business owner is reading this. The questions going through their mind are, "What's the process like? How do we get started? How do we pay this person? What's in it for us and for you?" Talk about that, in terms of helping people understand why

	they should seek you out. Talk about what people will be missing if they didn't engage you or somebody like you and they try to go on their own.
Ken:	People think about their homes as their largest asset. And typically, they'll buy and sell several homes in their life. But if you're a business owner, that's your most important asset. That's supplying the income to provide for your family, put a roof over their head, send your kids to college, and do all the things you need to do. And most people will only sell a business once in their lifetime. So the first thing to do is make sure you're doing it right. Unfortunately, it's way more difficult than most people understand. If they're in the middle of it, they're probably by themselves or probably pulling their hair out.

The other thing is there are other people who will come on and say, "Well, I can sell your business for you." The problem is those other people who dabble in it, don't know how to properly market the business. They don't know how to do it confidentially. Most people don't do it confidentially. They'll put themselves out there on Craigslist or something like that. I've seen them just put a For Sale sign in the window.

Unfortunately, there's a stigma that's associated whenever a business owner chooses to sell their business. And it's unfortunate, because as a business owner, nobody says anything if you decide to sell your car, your house, or anything, but the minute you're going to sell your business, everyone wonders why.

Whether you choose me or someone else, what tyou need to do is work specifically with somebody who knows the ins and outs of selling a business. How to engage buyers. How to market your business confidentially. And if you meet with them early, like you should, that can help you structure the sale. Because everybody focuses on price, but realistically it's not so much about what you sell the business for, it's how much you get to keep. So, in that process, you might find different benefits or pitfalls. As business intermediators, we have all kinds of resources to be able to direct a seller. Just to say, "Okay, go talk to this individual," or, "Hey, we're going to sell the business! You're going to have X amount left over. If you don't have a financial planner, maybe I can refer you to some I work with." Or "Maybe this individual needs a different CPA or somebody who's a little bit more skilled in this particular industry than this one." And you start to get all that information out early instead of later and answer any of their questions.

In terms of the process, really the first thing that needs to be done is, you need to establish the price. That's on the business, and the real estate, if it's owned. What's it worth? Many times, a business owner has a vague estimate. They may be correct, but often they're way off. There are reasons for that, because when it comes to the valuation on businesses, there's so much wrong information out there. People come many times with misinformation. I've been told, "It's two-times the annual earnings." I've heard, "It's a five-times multiple on X." Part of that might be right over here, and part might be right over there, but there's not one way to do it. Every business is different.

Valuation is more of an art than a science, and there are other factors that people don't take into account. The volatility of one industry compared to the stability of another, and how the metrics play into that. So, that's the other thing. When people take a business, and try to do it on their own, and the price isn't correct, it's very easy to get defensive. But the other side of that is, you need to, as I say, throw your buyer's hat on and look at it through the lens of a buyer, how they're seeing your business. And that's the other reason why working with us helps bring that expectation down.

In terms of the process, once the pricing is put in place, we engage them as a client. Some of that is probably similar in fashion to a real estate transaction. We're going to have an engagement agreement. We're going to market the business for a period of time. We're going to pre-qualify buyers. We have a very effective proprietary marketing system, and basically it just floods out to a series of websites we have. Which is another reason it's different using a national firm like us versus an independent. Because a lot of times, an independent has to take on all that stuff themselves.

We have established relationships. We have a whole department that does the marketing, instead of just me. If I was by myself, I'd say, "Okay, I just got this engagement. Now, let's see. I want to market here, here, here and here. And I've got to do that over there, and I've got to maintain those." But I can do all my work and send it out, and they're going to take it from there. We typically don't have any problems finding buyers for businesses.

Roger: It sounds great. You referenced the quality of life up here. There are probably a lot of people who are looking to buy businesses that a seller wouldn't be able to find without someone like you. Maybe people want to escape California, or wherever, and they're looking to come up here and be an entrepreneur, so you're able to have those resources, as well.

Ken: Yes! Especially in my area, there's a lot of out-of-state activity. In Coeur d'Alene you get a large influx of tourism in the summertime. How many countless times I've heard people who are living there now say things like, "20 years ago we drove through here on our honeymoon, and just loved the place and said we would come back one day", and they do. Or, young families who are looking to leave for a better place, and they want to buy a business. It's an area that I don't have to work very hard to sell.

Roger: Absolutely. Is there anything you would like to share that I didn't hit on, which you feel is important for people to know?

Ken: I would say it's to educate yourself a little bit on the industry. Know there's a reason why we exist, and it's really to the benefit of the buyer and the seller. I think, especially with the seller. I've tried to share some of my pains and my own experience in selling my own without representation, because a lot of that was unknown to me at the time. So I've really tried to help as much as I can with other people who are looking at doing the same thing and to really understand there's a lot more to this than you think.

Roger: I would imagine sellers really appreciate that, when you say, "I started in this because of my own experiences in selling a business." Do they gravitate toward that?

Ken: Yes, that's the "Why" people would talk about. I can really empathize with somebody when I'm meeting with them, if they're burned out or struggling or whatever. It's important, wherever someone is reading this book, we have a network of brokers across the country, so there's bound to be somebody in your vicinity that can assist you. And even if you chose another firm over us, it's important to maintain the confidentiality and understand how the numbers come in and how it all interconnects with yourself, the business, and the buyer. It's very important.

Roger: I imagine similar to my business, at the end of the process you often hear people say, "I had no idea," about the complexities we're dealing with. And there's probably a lot of appreciation for what you've done.

Ken: Yes, which is why I go through that in such detail at the beginning. For example, I'm working on a deal now where the lender is SBA funded, which is bogging things down a little. The seller is getting a little frustrated. I just have remind both parties, "This is something you both want to happen. This is just part of the process." I try to explain things like that in the beginning. But things can still pop out that I didn't even think would be an issue. We just have to work through it because we're trying to get to the same common goal. "You guys want to retire. These people are excited about buying your business. Let's not lose sight of that and get through it." There are just so many parts of it.

Roger: I've enjoyed getting to know you better, and I look forward to having a resource now I can send people to. Because I have clients that need to start getting on the sale of their business so they can make a proper exit.

Ken: It's really a lot larger than most people think. It's one of the last things they think about, until the time comes and they find out, "Okay, I'm ready to go. What do you mean it's going to take at least a year to sell my business? People will be lining up for this." As I've said, there are a lot of things that happen in the process, and it's not a quick turn. I'd say, typically we're running at least 12 months right now, for a business to actually get to the market and sell.

Roger: So it's important to get out in front of it! Ken, thank you for this valuable information.

To Contact Ken:
https://murphybusiness.com/
13403 N. Government Way, Ste 201
Hayden, Idaho 83835
Phone: (208) 449-1117

Chapter 9
DIANE GARDNER

Diane Gardner is the founder of Adept Business Services in Rathdrum, ID. She is a licensed Enrolled Agent, a Certified Profit First Professional, an Accredited Tax Preparer and has elite certification as a Certified Tax Coach. Diane saves her small business clients between $5,000 and $50,000.

She is the co-author of the best-selling books, *Stand Apart* and *Why Didn't My CPA Tell Me That?* and has authored six other books including, *Stop Overpaying Your Taxes! 11 Ways Entrepreneurs Overpay and How to Stop it Now!*

Diane created the nationwide *Get Off the Wheel - Practice Management Solutions for Accountants,* and leads the *Business Breakthrough Mastermind Group* in Rathdrum.

Roger: Diane Gardner is an enrolled agent and certified tax coach. Diane, here we are doing an interview for a book and I couldn't help noticing that when I walked into your lobby you're displaying a number of books you've written. Why don't we start with those?

Diane: I think I have eleven now. Several years ago, my business coach told me, "If you're ever going to be anybody you've got to write a book." So, I took that to heart, and not knowing what to do at the beginning, I jumped into a couple co-authored books as a way to get my feet wet.

From there, I went ahead and wrote a few more books and just continued to expand as the need arises. It's nice, because now I rarely carry business cards. I carry my books and they don't get thrown away.

Roger: That's tremendous. Of the books you've written, is there one that's your particular favorite?

Diane: My favorite is *Stop Overpaying Your Taxes*.

Roger: I could probably jump right in there with you. Nobody likes to overpay taxes.

Diane: Nobody likes to overpay, and I like to work with my clients to come up with a plan so I can get them some free money back from the government.

Roger: Tell me a little about your business here. What areas do you specialize in? What would be your banner you'd raise to say, "This is what we do for our clients. This is the type of service we offer"?

Diane: We like to lead off with our tax planning services. We work with successful business owners all across the nation. We have clients from Rhode Island to Hawaii. And in working with them, we're able to set up a plan to help them into a lower income tax liability by utilizing court tested, IRS approved strategies straight out of the IRS code.

These are things most people aren't even aware they're missing out on, because they don't know what they don't know. So we're able to set up a plan. Then, a lot of times as part of the maintenance of that plan, they need bookkeeping, or they need their taxes prepared or they need payroll processed or whatever. We can handle that part too, but we love to do the tax planning.

As an aside, we also love to work with people who are selling properties, homes, businesses, or commercial properties. Whatever it might be. Because we have some awesome tax-saving strategies that allow you to put a big chunk of that money you would have paid in income tax, back in your pocket and not have to give that to the government.

Roger: Is there a particular one of those strategies that comes to mind that you'd like to share?

Diane: Well, my most favorite one is anybody who's selling a property over about $550,000, that has a lot of gain in it, whether you're selling a business or a piece of property, whether it's a home or commercial real estate. We're able to defer the tax on that sale for 30 years. By deferring the tax, they were able to take a small amount of the money and invest it so the money's there to pay the tax in 30 years. You then walk away with almost all the money coming out of escrow, instead of leaving about half of it on the table for the IRS.

Roger: I had no idea. Is that through a private letter ruling or something like that? Straight out of code?

Diane: Straight out of the code, but most accountants and tax preparers are not familiar with that section of the code. I don't do those myself, I work with another company who has the attorneys and everybody behind them to make this happen for people.

Because otherwise, about half of it will go to the government between federal and state depending where you are. And that's painful.

Roger: Very interesting. Here we are in Rathdrum, Idaho, a small town north of Coeur d'Alene. You referenced working with clients all across the country. You probably didn't start that way. How did you get started in this business and grow to having clientele all over the country?

Diane: It all started with writing that first book. Once that book was written it started opening the door to some seminars. I'm an accountant and I really was uncomfortable with that. I had to learn how to do it. It was very painful for me, but I've done it.

Then from there, I started getting interviewed, especially once books two and three and four came along. Those interviews opened the door to working nationwide. Which is great, because I was struggling to find enough people in Rathdrum, Idaho who need tax planning services. This is not an affluent community. So we decided to fish in a bigger pond.

Roger: I love that story. So you started gathering clients across the country. Is there a particular vein of businesses you work with or is it very broad?

Diane: It's somewhat broad. I love to work with doctors, and professionals, and service businesses. I think those are the ones who get hammered the hardest on taxes. Those are some of my favorites, but of course I work with others as well.

And we have local clients too. In fact, we just moved into an office that's twice the size of our previous office, because we've grown so much.

Roger: How long have you been in the accounting business?

Diane: 24 years in Idaho and 13 in California. But I'm only 29 years old.

Roger: I might need an accountant to do the math on that one. It's a pleasure to be here in a brand-new office. It's a beautiful building and it smells brand new. You must have done a lot of work getting in here.

Diane: Yes, they've been working on it for five months. It actually used to be a bar. We're pretty proud of how it came out. This tax season as people come through the door, they're going to stop and say, "Wow, what happened in here?" Because people knew this building for what it was. In fact, when we were looking for a bigger space and my husband came across this one I thought, "No, not that building."

Roger: That's great. So this is a financial planning book, with a focus of letting people know what advice is out there and where they can go for that advice. Let's say someone reading this has accumulated some assets, or has a small business, and they're trying to do their taxes on their own. Why should they bother coming in and seeing somebody like you?

Diane: It's too bad they can't see my facial expression. The reason they should see somebody like me is because you don't know what you don't know. You probably know your business well, or maybe you've gotten good at your investments, but you don't know the tax code. You don't know those changes that happen that are wrapped up in certain bills that are never, ever promoted in the news. It's a side note that got attached to a particular bill. Like the tanning tax that got attached to the ACA about 10 years ago when that one first came out. Nobody realized tanning salons were going to pay a 10% excise tax that was hidden in there. Reasons like that are why you want to be in with a professional accountant.

And not just any kind of accountant, but somebody who's proactive. Most accountants are awesome at recording history. They'll tell you what you did last year, the year before, and the year before that. They'll put all the numbers in the right spaces on the right forms and file it on time, but then they stop. They don't go any further. But somebody who's proactive will then help you set up a plan for the future, and help you monitor it. They'll make sure you're meeting your goals and that things are happening the way you want them to happen in your total financial life. Not just your business or just one piece of it. We work in conjunction with the financial planners to make sure things are happening the way they're supposed to.

Roger: Good. What occurred in your career to cause you to become a proactive planner like that? Was there something that came along?

Diane: Prior to the recession, I was more of your typical accountant. During that time period I had clients going out of business right and left. They were so affected by that recession, and by the housing industry slumping the way it did. I had just bought my previous building in 2007 at the top of the market and dumped a ton of money into cleaning it up. So I was scared to death of what was I going to do. With my clients going out of business, I obviously needed to find new clients who were more insulated from the ups and downs of the economy. So I started looking for ways to do that. In my search, I came upon this group that was helping train accountants and tax preparers how to do proactive tax planning. I thought, "This makes sense, go after the people who have money." Now we're known for our tax planning services all across the nation.

Roger: It all fits together, becoming proactive and wanting to write your books. You've built a practice that you're obviously proud of, and you enjoy coming to work. Have you seen your proactive approach influence the way other people run their businesses?

Diane: Yes, I have. I have clients all over that have implemented my proactive approach. For example, a client here in Northern Idaho who was my very first tax plan. After meeting with him and preparing a customized tax plan, his tax savings have been between $30,000 and $35,000 a year for the last several years. He has purchased and completely paid for his commercial building. Prior to that he was renting. So that was part of our strategy. He wanted an asset out there for retirement. He was very disciplined, so he started putting his extra-estimated IRS into a savings account, and was able to buy his building and then pay it off within about three years instead of 30.

Roger: Excellent. Without betraying confidentiality, are you able to share details about how you were able to proactively identify the areas where he could save that much money?

Diane: Yes I can. For one thing we looked at his entity type. He had really outgrown that, so we were able to switch him into an entity that worked better for the stage he was at in business. That saved him about $10,000 to $15,000 a year.

Then we looked at some retirement planning for him and we were able to come up with a retirement plan that fit his needs, for not only him and his family, but also for his employees. That probably saved him close to another $15,000 a year from there. Then we implemented a bunch of little things, to keep him averaging between $30,000 and $35,000 a year.

Roger: You saved a client money, and changed families' lives by putting retirement plans in place.

Diane: Yes, and with this we worked hand-in-hand with a financial planner in Coeur d'Alene to put this all together for him. We took care of the legwork and the paperwork side of it, so all my client had to do was show up and sign.

Roger: How did you cross paths? Did he come into you as a referral?

Diane: He was a brand-new client who came in with a sales tax audit issue, which was completely unrelated from what we ended up doing for him.

Roger: So you rescued him from that and then got proactive. You changed his life, along with a bunch of other people.

Diane: And when I told him about it, I said, "I just started on a new area in business. Will you let me practice on you?" He said, "Well, okay." He wasn't sure about that. Which I can understand. He was new to me, and I was telling him I've never done this before. But it definitely worked out.

I have lots of those kinds of stories. Another example is a local author. We met at one of my book signing events. Through his tax planning, they've gone from renting a home to building their dream home. Owning a home was always one of their big dreams. They wanted their kids to have a big back yard and all that kind of stuff. So he built their home two years ago. It's very cool to me when I see they've got this house sitting there now. It's not completely paid for, but every year his tax savings allow him to pay it down faster than they would otherwise.

Roger: I imagine those type of things would probably fall under a description you said earlier, "People don't know what they don't know."

So you get engaged, you start to learn about this person's life, and then you're able to start teaching and start to recreate the way they're running their money.

Diane: That's right. It all depends on what their goal is. When I work with my clients for tax planning, I have a little questionnaire that has about 10 or 15 things on it, and I have them rank the items by levels of importance from a one to a five.

Then depending on what they say is important to them, that's how we start inputting the other plan and structuring it. In this particular author's case, they wanted a home before they wanted to start putting stuff away for retirement, so we did the home part first. Now it's time to come back and visit with him and say, "Okay, now it's time to start looking at putting together a retirement plan."

It's neat to see, because everybody has different goals. So I work within their goal structure and make sure I have a team that I can go to. Whether it's an attorney, financial planners, whoever I need to go to and say, "Here's somebody that needs X, Y, and Z." Then making sure it happens.

Roger: So you do a lot of teaming. I do quite a bit of that too. What are some of the other things that would fall under that category of, "people don't know what they don't know?" Our tax code is something like 72,000 pages. What are some of the big things where you have those "A-ha" moments for your clients?

Diane: Some of the favorite ones are when I can show somebody how they can write off 100% of all their out-of-pocket medical through their business, because that's money they're spending anyhow. If I can move it from a nondeductible place to a deductible place on their tax return, it may only be saving them $4,000 or $5,000 a year, but that's $4,000 or $5,000 a year they didn't have before.

There are things like hiring their kids or hiring their parents to work in their business. They're helping them anyhow. They're giving them money anyhow. So why not see if we can structure it as a way we can write off legitimately through their business. Here again, put some more money back in your pocket. Pass some money down to lower tax brackets. You're helping them out financially anyhow, so let's make it deductible.

There are a lot of those kind of fun little strategies that we get to do, in addition to some of the bigger ones, which depend on the profitability of the business. We can get into more of the retirement planning and some of that stuff.

Roger: For people who are reading this book right now, who would be your ideal client? Who should come in and see you, or get in touch with you if they're in a different state?

Diane: Successful entrepreneurs who are in intense pain over the amount of taxes they're paying, or that have some real estate investments or something along those lines where we can structure a business entity around it.

If they're not in pain, then there's no reason to come see me. But if they're in pain because they hate writing that huge check to the IRS every year or those big, big massive estimated payments, most of the time we can change that.

Roger: Wonderful. Do you have any thoughts on things that are happening right now in terms of discussions regarding tax law changes?

Diane: The tax law that was signed into effect late in 2017 has really made some massive changes in our tax code. Some of the changes will benefit individuals and others will really benefit businesses. 2018 is an interesting year as we learn how to use the new tax law to save money for our clients.

Roger: We've covered quite a bit. Is there anything we haven't touched on that you feel might be important to share, either about what you do or what people should know about tax planning?

Diane: I think people need to realize that failing to plan is the biggest mistake they can make when it comes to their taxes. If they don't realize that they can plan their way to a lower tax liability, then they just take whatever shows up and they just pay it.

But if they realize they can plan their way to a lower liability, that opens up a whole world of "what ifs". What if we did this, what if we did that? How can we make this work in your situation? The money they can recoup back from overpaid taxes is wonderful.

We always say you need to pay your fair share of taxes, but there's nothing out there that says you have to leave the IRS a big tip.

Roger: Yes, not a penny more. I like that.

Diane: Not a penny more than what you have to pay. Everything we do is court tested and IRS approved.

Roger: Tremendous. On a personal note, here we live in God's country, what do you do outside the office?

Diane: I love to read. I'm not a "big crowds" kind of person. My husband and I like to get out in the woods, take a drive out in the hills somewhere with a picnic lunch. We love doing that kind of thing. I also love to spend time with my six-year-old grandson. He is so much fun to play with. We like to get out on the four-wheeler and do things with him. Other than that, just spending time with family.

Roger: Great. Diane this has been a pleasure. I look forward to reading some of your books, and I appreciate the wonderful addition you've made to mine.

RETIREMENT BASECAMP

To contact Diane:
Email: diane@taxcoach4you.com
Phone: (208) 687-0508 or (800) 841-0212
Mailing Address:
Diane Gardner
c/o Adept Business Solutions
PO Box 1132
14567 W. Highway 53
Rathdrum, ID 83858

CLOSING THOUGHTS

I hope you got as much out of reading these interviews as I did conducting them. This group of professionals sheds crucial light on areas of retirement planning that you may not have considered.

Part of building the right retirement is asking the right questions and having the right team in your basecamp to support your goals. I hope this book gets you thinking beyond the numbers and gets you thinking how you want to live the next chapter of your life.

By choosing to read this book, you've shown you're serious about making smart choices. And that is the foundation of a strong retirement plan, or any financial plan.

If I can help you in any way, my contact information is on the next page. I'm happy to meet with you for a Retirement Basecamp strategy session. No cost, no obligation, just a chance for me to answer your questions.

When you have a strong plan and the right support, the retirement summit is within your reach.

To Contact Roger Duval:
MassMutual Norwest
9 South Washington Street, Suite 405
Spokane, WA 99201
Office: (509) 842-511
Cell: (509) 869-2015
rogerduval@financialguide.com
CA Insurance License #0L06123

Proof

23437843R00117

Made in the USA
Columbia, SC
08 August 2018